André Gorz

Paths To Paradise

On The Liberation From Work

translated by Malcolm Imrie

Pluto Press

London and Sydney

Contents

Supplementary Texts / 79

Preface

The present crisis brings changes so profound and far-reaching that it can be compared to the first industrial revolution. We are living through the disintegration of a whole social system, a system which threatens to survive its own death by entombing us for decades in its own lifeless structures.* The weight of reality is dragging us towards a living-dead capitalism where the means of social production and social control can no longer be distinguished, where a normalising technocracy continues to glorify an already extinct order in the name of values which have long lost all meaning. No wonder, then, that the Soviet Union, that other dead star, holds such a fascination for Western technocracies: it provides the very paradigm of a living-dead social order which, unable to function by the values and goals that define it, only endures by virtue of its system of control.

In such a situation, orthodoxies and 'realism' are equally deadly. The present crisis breaks the continuity of two centuries of history, marked by the expansion of industrialism and the spread of commodity relations. And it compels us to abandon our long-cherished hopes and perspectives. To do so, we do not need to look for models in pre-capitalist societies. The perspectives that were adopted by the early workers' movement are acutely relevant today. For we are now reaching precisely the point that was foreseen by the first prophets of post-capitalism** when, beyond

---

* See theses 11 and 16 below.
** Notably Ricardo and his followers, and later Marx. It is impossible to understand the meaning of the present crisis without them – which does not mean that marxist theory is sufficient, or beyond criticism. See theses 7, 13 and 14 below.

bourgeois society and nascent industrial capitalism, they predicted a different social order – one where the efficacy of technology would abolish work, the logic of capital and commodity relations, to reveal 'disposable time' as the measure of 'true wealth'.

The micro-electronic revolution is pulling us in that direction, but the inertia of our own mental categories blinds us to the truth: we wait, forlornly, for the future to give us back the past, for the economic 'revival' or 'recovery' that will provide full employment, for capitalism to rise from its death-bed, for automation to create more jobs than it eliminates.

It is hardly surprising that the Right should thus deny or disguise the death of a world. But when the Left, in Europe and America, can conceive of no solution to the crisis other than state-managed capitalism, and still looks to Keynes for remedies which, already ineffective under Roosevelt, have become inapplicable, then it is clearly about to die from lack of imagination. There are times when, because the social order is collapsing, realism consists not of trying to manage what exists but of imagining, anticipating and initiating the potential transformations inscribed in present changes.*

This book is intended as a contribution to that process. In an attempt at concision, the first section is set out in the form of a series of theses. These are illustrated, explored and developed in the supplementary texts which follow them.

---

*See theses 17 to 25 below.

Twenty-five theses towards understanding the crisis and finding a Left solution

I. What's gone forever

1. Changing the future

Times of crisis are also times of great freedom. Our world is out of joint; societies are disintegrating, our lifelong hopes and values are crumbling. The future ceases to be a continuation of past trends. The meaning of present development is confused; the meaning of history suspended.

Because the curtain has fallen on the old order and no other order waits in the wings, we must improvise the future as never before. Those who propose a fundamentally different society can no longer be condemned in the name of realism. On the contrary, realism now consists of acknowledging that 'industrialism'[1] has reached a stage where it can go no further, blocked by obstacles of its own making. If nothing can go on as before, it is because of all that *has* gone on before. There can be no piecemeal solutions; the obstacles will only be overcome by overall restructuring, total transformation.

The direction which this restructuring and transformation will take is not predetermined, though certain tendencies are already clear. Several 'ways out' remain possible, several kinds of post-capitalist, post-socialist society. The direction of our escape from the crisis is the fundamental issue. It depends on political, technological and cultural choices – choices which we must now make.

2. Perceiving the crisis

The present crisis – but not the date when it would erupt – could be foreseen from the time when President Johnson proudly pro-claimed capitalism's capacity to guarantee perpetual growth and prosperity. It could be foreseen not only because no system can grow indefinitely, but also because the American economy's difficulties in finding consumers for increasing production were already manifest. In this respect, American involvement in Vietnam played a 'conjunctural support' role that has not always been clearly understood.

Yet the ideology of perpetual growth was so deeply rooted that any questions as to its pertinence or its desirability were taken by the Right as signs of ill-founded catastrophism, by the Left as hostility to 'progress'. Even since, both Right and Left have continued to try and manage the crisis as if it were a temporary disturbance. In three months, in a year, they predict the economic 'recovery' that will assure a return to growth and a reduction in unemployment. Even at the beginning of the summer of 1982, the French Prime Minister was promising that his anti-inflation plan 'would not halt growth'. He seemed unaware of the fact that this was now no higher than 0.5 per cent per annum, or that production was decreasing throughout the industrialised world.

The way we perceive the present crisis is itself one of the issues. For by its very reality, this crisis raises questions as to the adequacy of past politics, the primacy of the economic, the legitimacy of the ideologies and protagonists of dominant politics, be they of Right or Left. The crisis reveals that the workings of the economy are not controlled, or even understood, by its managers and functionaries. Our societies are not masters of their own future. While living through their collapse, we are fed with promises that tomorrow we will rediscover the hopes of 15 years ago – however forlorn they have since become. All dominant ideologies combine to prevent us seeing this crisis as the end of the industrialist era and the possible beginning of another, founded on a different rationale, different values and relationships, a different life.

3. Changing socialism

To talk of an industrialist civilisation is not to ignore or deny its essentially capitalist character. The fact that industrialism is common to both capitalism and socialism emphasises the importance and the implications of this notion. The crisis too is common to capitalism and socialism, in so far as 'actually existing socialism' resembles a split-off from capitalism. Wherever socialism has come to power (with one exception, which I will come to later), its first endeavour has always been to accumulate and concentrate capital faster than capitalism. For in none of the countries that we call socialist – with the same single exception – had primitive accumulation, bourgeois revolution or 'industrial revolution' taken place when socialism was established. The exception is Czechoslovakia.[2] And that is undoubtedly why opposition to 'actually existing socialism' in Czechoslovakia has been in the name of a different and more advanced concept of socialism, and not, as in almost all the other socialist European countries, only in the name of basic freedoms.

It is significant that East Germany, the most industrialised country in the Eastern bloc, and one of the most heavily industrialised regions in the world, has produced, with Rudolf Bahro, an eco-socialist opposition, which challenges the productivism and industrialism of Western civilisation.[3]

Future socialism will be post-industrial and anti-productivist or it will not be. Its definition is another fundamental issue, on a world scale, that is, beyond the frontiers of the three worlds.

4. Changing development

Socialist industrialism does not contain the answer to the present crisis or to the hunger and poverty of the Third World, any more than capitalist industrialism, whose more rational copy it wants to be.[4] Neither can be extended on a planetary scale, so destructive are they of limited natural resources and balances necessary for the continuation of life itself.*

The solution to the specific problems of the under-nourished world depends on the industrialised world adopting a model of consumption and production that is less wasteful, less ostentatious, and which generates less dependence, enabling people to be more capable of producing what they consume. The argument that we owe it to the under-nourished countries to persevere with industrialism and productivism in order to provide them with the

---

* See Supplementary Text, II. 'Their famine, our food'.

industries they urgently need is false and hypocritical. Hunger and poverty in the Third World are not a result of 'backwardness' or of inadequate productive forces. Instead they are a result of:

1. The draining of their resources by the industrialised, capitalist countries;
2. The political and social obstacles to the utilisation of their own productive forces (for which colonialism and latterly the neo-colonialism of the multinationals are largely responsible).

It is enough to know that the level of unemployment, in all the under-nourished countries, is between 20 and 60 per cent (in general a low estimate, since it does not take account of the under-employment of peasant smallholders) in order to see the most urgent problem: to enable the populations to produce their subsistence with tools that can be readily made and used *on the spot*. The answer is not to sell ready-made factories on credit to their governments, factories which will pay Western salaries to Western-trained technicians while allowing a derisory proportion of the population to become wage-labourers and imitate an American model (but not level) of consumption.

The idea of a 'European Marshall Plan' that would off-load in the Third World industrial surplus that has become unsaleable elsewhere is a crude swindle: to 'give work' (thank you very much, sir!) to European workers, it would supply labour-saving devices and technologies to countries where there is neither land, work nor means of production for 20, 40, 60 per cent of the population. What would these plants make, and who would buy it? Above all, obviously, consumer products, for consumers (including the unemployed) in the rich countries. For there certainly are not enough solvent consumers in the poor countries – not even enough to buy the produce of lands hoarded by estate owners and multinationals.

All the international aid and development organisations (the UN, UNESCO, UNICEF, the World Bank, etc.) have had to recognise in recent years that hunger and poverty will not be eliminated by economic growth of the industrialist type, but only by policies aimed specifically at giving the widest possible sections of the population access to the means of self-production (notably land) and thus to self-production itself.[5] The development of this,

and of appropriate technologies in the industrial countries themselves – including the cultural changes that it promotes – will be of
greater help to the people of the Third World than the sale on
credit of cement works and nuclear reactors.

One of the central issúes of the crisis is whether or not the
pre-industrial world will be given the chance to move into a
post-industrial and post-capitalist mode of production without
going through the generalisation of wage and market relations
specific to industrialism.[6]

II. Understanding the crisis

5. Keynes

The present crisis is not a temporary interruption of economic growth, but a *consequence* of it. In fact, how we explain the crisis is part of what is at issue, for this will determine how we try to overcome it, and with what aim.

Since the crisis began, the quality of the explanations for it has declined alarmingly. But this is hardly a new phenomenon. For just as marxist-inspired analysis was capable of interpreting the warning signs and forecasting a deep and protracted crisis, so the self-proclaimed marxist and socialist political parties have been incapable of defining a policy which could overcome it by breaking from the logic of capitalism.

Their incapacity is not surprising. Economic systems are not transformed by acts of government. The economic machinery which capitalism installed but can no longer operate will not function any better under ostensibly socialist management. As we shall see, the causes of the crisis are so deeply embedded in the structure of the productive system that their elimination depends on reconstructing the system, not managing it.

But the self-proclaimed socialist parties have not had sufficient perception, or courage, to say so openly. Wherever they have held power, or anticipated holding power, they have believed it possible to treat this crisis as a problem of under-consumption, demanding classical, Keynesian-inspired solutions. Yet Keynesian policies, wherever they were implemented, have failed either to prevent or reduce unemployment (although in Austria and Sweden they have temporarily delayed its rise).

This failure, which, as we shall show, was also predictable, has discredited a 'socialism' which has come to identify itself with a Keynesian management of capitalism. Thanks to the crisis of

Keynesian social democracies, neo-liberalism has been able to launch an all-out ideological offensive under the themes of 'the bankruptcy of socialism' and 'market capitalism – the response to the crisis'. The theses which follow will deal with the reasons for the failure of Keynesianism.

6. The limits of Keynesian regulation

In the past, capitalism's periodic crises have had two principal causes:

1. over-accumulation, that is, the investment of amounts of capital in excess of what can be made profitable by the sale of realisable production at market price;
2. under-consumption, that is, the inability of part of the population to satisfy its potential demand because of lack of purchasing power.

Over-accumulation and under-consumption are obviously linked. The former would not occur, or would at least be delayed, if potential demand (broadly speaking, from the poor) could be realised. To do so, and thus to expand the market, means of payment must be distributed to potential consumers, through taxes on high incomes and, especially, on company profits.

State taxes on company profits and their redistribution as social expenditure, subsidies and public investments assume a far greater strategic importance than the redistribution of part of private incomes. For they ensure that *total profits do not exceed the opportunities for profitable investment*. They prevent the market from collapsing after a period of over-investment, with all the destruction of capital that would entail through a series of company closures and stock liquidations.

Keynesian policies, then, are acts of *external regulation*, performed by state technocracy to compensate for the market economy's own inadequate capacity for self-regulation. They are in the overall interest of capitalism as a system – but they clash with the interests of individual capitalists, of particular firms, since compulsory contributions and taxes reduce the size of their potential profits before these have even been realised. Each individual firm is led to believe that it would make a far greater profit without state intervention, while in fact insufficient demand and lack of opportunity for profitable investment would rapidly produce a substantial drop in realisable profits.

However, *Keynesian regulation can work only during times of high profits, of strong potential growth, and thus of strong propensity to invest. It can regulate and sustain economic growth, but cannot, alone, create the conditions for it.* It cannot instigate growth when a long cycle of accumulation comes to an end, and when, through market saturation, labour shortage and exhaustion of the resources of technological progress, the rate of profit falls and a long downward cycle begins. We shall return to this point later.

At best, Keynesian regulation can soften the effects of a structural depression, but only at the cost of a sharper fall in the rate of profit and/or higher inflation. It can never eliminate the structural causes of the crisis. On the contrary, these are clear signs that capitalist development, along with its Keynesian regulation, has reached its limit.

7. The falling rate of profit and class struggle

The exhaustion of economic growth and the advent of a depressive cycle had been noted from the mid-1960s by marxist economists (in particular, Ernest Mandel and, from a different perspective, Paul Sweezy and the *Monthly Review*). The profitability of what had been expanding industries declined, especially in the United States and West Germany, speeding up the 'multinationalisation' of major companies, that is, the setting up of subsidiaries in countries with low rates of pay.[1]

At the beginning of the 1970s, French economists, in particular, drew attention to the 'fall in the marginal productivity of capital': in other words, to the fact that production was growing at a lower rate than capital investment. In itself, this is not necessarily alarming: the growth of production is not the obligatory goal of investment. But when the divergence between these two rates of growth widens over several years, it acquires considerable significance: it reveals that the production system is *using increasing amounts of capital per unit of output*. Economists would say that production is thus becoming 'capital intensive'. And from about

1965, this development had a clear aim: to replace workers by machinery, labour by capital.

In France, between 1960 and 1974, the rate of increase in productive investment was thus on average one-third higher than in production. Productive fixed capital per worker rose by 5.5 per cent a year between 1964 and 1973: it increased by a multiple of 2.6 in 20 years.[2] The tendency that Marx (within quite different parameters) described as 'the rise in organic composition of capital', was thus borne out: capital invested in the means of production ('fixed capital') was taking on an increasing weight in relation to labour costs (or 'circulating capital').[3]

Now when an increasing amount of fixed capital is utilised per unit of output, the rate of profit can remain constant only if the productivity *of labour* rises proportionately. For its own reproduction (to cover depreciation), a company must consume a greater part of its earnings and consequently its labour force must consume a smaller part. In other words, the *rate of exploitation* has to increase in parallel with labour productivity. The new machinery, *when it is more costly than the old*, can only be equally profitable if it allows a reduction in the total amount of wages per unit of output. Otherwise, the rate of profit will fall.

Of course, this fall is not mathematically necessary, any more than is the rise in the organic composition of capital. Against a fatalistic marxism which sees capitalism digging its grave by the mere logic of its own immanent laws, several radical economists have recently proved that neither a rise in organic composition nor a fall in the rate of profit are inherently necessary to the capitalist mode of production, and, further, that the former can occur without the latter.[4]

Indeed, there is no *mathematical* necessity for capitalism to replace labour by machinery and, when it does, it is not mathematically necessary for the new, improved machinery to have a higher capital cost per unit of output than the old. On the contrary, capitalist growth can be 'extensive' rather than 'capital intensive': it can be based on an increase in the number of machines *and* workers, without substituting the former for the latter. And where this substitution occurs, new machinery can provide a higher output *without its cost rising* proportionately. In fact, a sensible capitalist would only install it if this was the case, *as long as there was still a choice*: normally one buys new machinery only if it can reduce the unit cost of production and provide a better return on investment.

In practice, however, capitalist development does not always go according to plan – and will always lead to situations where capital loses control of events. The conditions which allowed it to expand the economy according to its own internal logic are eventually eroded by the very effects of this expansion. At first, capital is forced to make decisions which would *normally* be irrational. Inevitably, this is followed by a period of crisis in which, through major changes, the past is written off and the base prepared for a new period of growth.

At the beginning of the present crisis, capital lost control of its own development for two basic reasons: labour supplies were exhausted, and technological progress was levelling off. The former is a perfect example of the 'external' physical constraints that economic science tends to overlook: decision-makers ignore it in their regular forecasts. But when there is full employment, and when labour shortages are starting to bite, 'extensive' growth is out of the question. Capitalism no longer has any alternative. If it is to prevent economic growth from grinding to a halt, it must substitute capital (machinery) for labour. And this substitution is all the more urgent when full employment sets up a balance of forces that favours the workers: the pressure of their demands intensifies, their reliability and productivity drop.

In this situation, any considerations about the overall advantages of the new machinery which will replace human labour become secondary. For this replacement is now seen as an urgent necessity. But without long-term planning and forecasting, there is every likelihood that it will be misconceived. The cost of the new machinery will tend to be proportionately greater, per unit of output, than that of the old: machine manufacture is a traditional stronghold of skilled workers and it is there that labour shortage and workers' demands will have most impact. And in most cases the new machinery is not readily accepted by the workers who are required to operate it. Anticipated gains in productivity are often a long time coming.

So without a technological breakthrough which substantially reduces the cost of machinery (that is, the amount of fixed capital per unit of output) there will be a sharp rise in organic composition. At the same time, because of workers' resistance, the rise in labour productivity is not enough to achieve the usual rate of profit on productive equipment that is now more costly per unit of output. A falling rate of profit is inevitable.

As many marxist-inspired economists have recently shown,[5] it is thus clear that the falling rate of profit and the rise in organic composition are linked to the success of class struggle. More precisely, they are linked to capital's incapacity, when growth is blocked by full employment, to raise productivity – *including productivity in machine manufacture* – fast enough to prevent the substitution of capital for labour being paid for by a drop in profitability. From 1965, with the effects of full employment, only a technological breakthrough would have been able to prevent the balance of forces between labour and capital moving in favour of the former.

The shortage of labour in this period quickly pushed up wages. Employers responded by trying to speed up work: workers rejected this, first by passive resistance, later by militant direct action. With existing technology, it proved impossible to increase labour productivity, contrary to expectations. In the United States, then in West Germany, Italy, Britain, France and Sweden, workers' rejection of the ever-increasing fragmentation and speeding-up of work showed itself in sabotage, wildcat strikes, high absenteeism and a labour turnover of over 35 per cent. Reconstructing the assembly-line division of labour and introducing new machinery become emergency operations: the rapid rise in wages has already cut into profits, and workers' militancy is causing serious disruptions.

But emergency innovations do not give the desired results. Like the Fiat plant in Turin and Ford factories in Britain, General Motors' new factory in Lordstown in the southern United States, opened in 1969, is a typical case. The workers, most of them young and from semi-rural backgrounds, immediately rejected General Motors' neo-Taylorist organisation, and the factory, with its highly advanced design, could function only at a fraction of capacity for its first two years.

Faced with falling profits, the big companies choose headlong flight: setting up subsidiaries in the Third World, launching new product lines, investing in productivity and capacity. Banking on a future rise in demand, they go into debt at a time when the market is almost saturated and demand, without major innovations, is near its peak. The resulting growth and high inflation are the prelude to a structural downturn at the start of the 1970s.

So the success of class struggle has been a determining factor in the genesis of the crisis. But while the labour movement has managed to thwart the logic of capitalism, it has failed to replace it. Indeed, even when the crisis had come to a head and it seemed that only a chance event was needed to trigger the downturn, the French Left was still advocating faster growth. In the 1973 parliamentary elections, still faithful to the myth of eternal growth, the Socialists promised an 8 per cent annual growth rate, as opposed to 5 – 6 per cent.

In short, the Left remained obsessed with Keynesian blueprints while capitalism was already heading into a new long-term crisis: all sources of growth were exhausted. Markets were saturated; profitability of investments was insufficient (in the United States the rate of self-financing had fallen below 40 per cent in 1974); costs of wages and benefit contributions, along with the price of raw materials, were rising inexorably; overcapacities began to show in what had previously been the fastest-growing industries. Only a major technological breakthrough and a shift in capital's favour of the balance of social forces could permit a new growth cycle.

Of course this does not mean that, without militant class struggle, the period of growth would have continued indefinitely. Infinite growth of material production is a material impossibility. Growth will always reach a structural limit: its specific sources are never inexhaustible. But this limit will become evident only through complex circumstantial and conjunctural causes, as the expression of a balance of social forces, as the end of a particular history.[6]

8. The impossible revival

The structural causes of the crisis explain the failure of all attempts at 'reviving growth'. 'Reflation through demand' ran up against the saturation of the market for what had previously been key products: cars and domestic appliances. Sales to those few homes not already fully equipped were restricted for reasons of culture, age or space rather than by lack of purchasing power. Not everyone enjoys music enough to want a stereo system; if you live in the centre of town, a car can be an inconvenience; not every home (or, especially, every kitchen) is spacious enough for a wide range of domestic appliances. The revival can only be differential and specific, but the areas where need is most obvious (home improvements and insulation, urban renewal, tree-planting and forestry, water treatment, etc.), are often those where demand can only be public and collective, requiring small-scale or labour-intensive enterprises, not capital-intensive industries. Thus we cannot expect a new cycle of accumulation and the kind of growth which feeds on rising profits.

Reflation through investment, on the other hand, faces two obstacles:

1. the existence of over-capacities and/or of an organic composition already so high that only the certainty of unusual gains in productivity would justify new investments;
2. computerisation and robotisation, which make possible these rises in productivity, but require the writing off of greater amounts of existing capital than the amounts newly invested, and destroy more jobs than they create. We shall return to this later.

Moreover, as neo-liberals always tell us, an investment revival depends on a revival of companies' capacity for self-financing, in other words, on a rise in their rate of profit. And this can be achieved only by cutting direct and indirect wage costs. The political difficulties of such cuts have been seriously under-estimated.

9. The vengeance of social costs

Capitalist growth has been based on maximising individual consumption. As we shall see, the extension of the state sector is both a prerequisite and a consequence of this maximisation. Contrary to the views of neo-liberals, such an extension has not hindered growth but rather been its necessary accompaniment. Cutting the state sector and its costs can be achieved only by changing the pattern of development and consumption. But such a change – which both Left and Right agree is inevitable – can be carried out in different ways, with different aims. Indeed, this is the central, if less recognised, issue in the present crisis.

Reducing the state sector by simply cutting off public expenditure seems impossible without a dictatorship, so vital are the two main functions of the institutions and policies of the Welfare State: *the production of order*, and *the production of the right type of demand* needed for capitalist development.[7]

Development of large-scale commercial production, with its mega-industries, mega-technologies and megalopolies, depends on a combination of infrastructures, networks and public services without which the production system could not work, reproduce itself or make the transformations and upheavals which it causes socially acceptable. These, in fact, are the *social costs* of capitalist development and they tend to rise with the expansion and concentration of industry. Meeting industry's labour requirements, in particular, means not only providing schooling and training for teenagers, but also employing formerly non-waged rural populations. Hence the need for programmes to modernise the rural areas, subsidise the concentration and mechanisation of farming, build homes for the displaced rural population, and socialise – through nurseries, kindergartens, school canteens, summer camps – the traditional functions of the family. Urbanisation and industrial concentration in turn demand new roads and public transport, telecommunications, health and sanitation services, etc.

Normally, there is no effective demand from individuals for these infrastructures, networks and services, nor are there private groups or firms able to develop and co-ordinate them on a national scale. In all such areas, public action and public finance are the condition – and often the prerequisite – of capitalist development. The state thus shoulders the burden of private industry's social costs. And it finances them by taxing incomes and company profits. While public expenditure is generally in the interest of private enterprise, it is in conflict with the particular interest of every private business.

The efficiency of public systems and services cannot be measured by the cost of what they produce. For what they produce is often less important than what they *prevent*: shortages, overcrowding, epidemics, irreparable damage, unacceptable side-effects, etc. The acceptability of the social effects of capitalist development and the system's political stability depend on the state paying the social costs.

We can judge the destructive effects of this development by the fact, among others, that one in two manual workers and one in three white collar workers becomes permanently unfit for work before retirement age; one manual worker in six and one white collar worker in ten does so before the age of 50.[8] Of course these are not all cases of total disability: the self-employed often stay active in situations where waged workers would be deemed disabled. Disability thus has a doubly social cause: it is linked to the increasing work load imposed upon waged workers. Men and women who, in a different social context, would be seen and would see themselves as perfectly fit, are dismissed from production because their performance is inadequate. Profit levels on invested capital depend on this exclusion of older workers – and the public bears the cost.

All reductions in public responsibility for social costs thus accentuate social inequalities and, especially, the *visibility* of these inequalities: the brutal elimination of the less fortunate by the better-off, the violence of social relations in the struggle for scarce resources (like air, space, light, cleanliness), the obscene privileges of wealth and power. Such reductions will accelerate the breakdown of social cohesion and will eventually lead to the collapse of state legitimacy and of a social order based on the rule of law.[9]

The public sector can thus be seen to have a role which is rarely recognised: it produces order, legitimacy and political stability. All reductions in public responsibility have 'destabilising' effects, and limit society's capacity to function with a minimum of physical violence.

The debate over the extent and form of public responsibility therefore raises a false issue. No political regime concerned about stability and legitimacy can afford substantially to reduce this responsibility.[10] The real issue of the crisis concerns what action to take to reduce *not the public responsibility for social costs but the social costs themselves*. Neither the Left nor the Right would challenge the need for such a reduction. Throughout the era of growth, social costs rose faster than overall production, and they continued to rise, albeit more slowly, when growth had come to a standstill. This cannot be seen as accidental, nor be explained by government laxity and demagogy, or the 'cost sickness' proposed by Baumol and Oates.[11] An increase in social costs shows that capitalist development has rising material and infrastructural costs ('organisation costs', properly speaking), but also that political stability and compensation for the upheavals caused by this development demand actions that are increasingly expensive and decreasingly productive.

The explanation must be sought in advanced capitalism's own model of development. Essentially this model derives from the principle that all problems and needs – even collective ones – must be answered by *individual* consumption of marketable goods and services. Growth of production and consumption depends on this quest for individual solutions to collective problems. But these individual solutions are more expensive than a collective response, and moreover are increasingly ineffective. The case has been systematically proved in the fields of housing, transport and health:

– Urbanisation based on the spread of detached-housing estates fosters the illusion of an individual answer to the shortage of space and accommodation in towns. The suburban estate is a negation of the town, offering each family the semblance of a private, 'semi-rural' solution to the accommodation crisis. The collective costs of such a solution start high, and keep rising as suburbia develops. Farming land and forests are destroyed, extensive public works are needed to supply water and energy, new road systems and fast public transport must be provided. The inevitable lack of communal facilities in the estates encourages private 'alternatives' (freezers, canned music and home videos, two- and three-car households), some of which (principally the cars) require additional, highly expensive development of public infrastructures: one kilometre of four-lane motorway costs as much as 10 kilometres of twin-track tramway moving twice as many passengers per hour.

– The health system based on more or less free access to *curative* care fosters the illusion that illnesses are accidents to be repaired by individual treatment. As Jacques Attali has shown,[12] keeping the labour force in working order and preventing premature losses, while boosting the legitimacy and stability of the Welfare State, was only the *initial* function of a state benefit scheme. Its symbolic role quickly replaced its protective one: it 'puts healing on show for the benefit of the healthy', a show which 'becomes the constituent element of individual consumption'.[13] In other words, it convinces everyone that illness has its source in the victim's body and can be treated individually. Healing, and indeed health itself, become commodities like any other: to be sold retail by professionals and wholesale by the makers of pharmaceuticals and hospital technology. State benefits resolve the only remaining problem – how to afford them. The social causes of diseases are ignored, even when their epidemiology has been understood for generations, and their elimination is clearly possible.[14]

The fact is that eliminating the *social* causes (notably work, housing and transport conditions; industrial pollution; alcoholism, smoking and commercially encouraged eating habits) would require public action on a collective scale. *Market exchange* of goods and services would have no role to play. Thus, instead of public health and hygiene, the state subsidises spectacular medicine – the virtuoso performances of intensive-care units with seemingly desperate cases. Welfarism will therefore have played a decisive role in the production of consumers and consumer ideology, and in conjuring away the collective reality of health problems. With the help of the state, it will have created individual commodity demand instead of collective control (through workers' and users' committees) and the capacity to care for ourselves and live a healthy life. It will have established clientism and dependency, thus reducing our power to control our own working conditions, lives and environment. As Bruno Jobert puts it:

> The characteristic response of social institutions to the stresses and strains of intolerable living conditions is to individualise the problem . . . They tend to place their clients in a position of permanent dependency on the services they offer, thus discouraging them from making a collective effort to change their own way of life.[15]

Public sector institutions, however, have their own dynamic which always tends to exceed functional requirements. It is this dynamic which explains the rising cost and falling effectiveness of social services. Health and education, especially, follow the same logic of 'progress' and 'catching up' as other forms of consumption: what is available to everyone is no longer good enough for the privileged. To meet their demand, something 'better' must be offered, which is available only to a minority. This will then quickly become the norm which the dominated classes strive to attain . . . and so on. Thus the poverty threshold keeps rising, but so do the levels of education and medical technique available to everyone.

But for all that, social inequality does not diminish, because every time the dominated classes advance, privilege is re-established at a higher level, thus devaluing their gains. So 'progress' in health and education becomes almost entirely illusory. The extension of education or the rise in so-called health costs no longer corresponds to any real progress: 'Health costs' share in the economic surplus has trebled in 20 years. And that of education costs has risen even faster. Yet . . . there has been no rise in life expectancy; half of all Americans cannot read or write at the age of 11.'[16]

For the Left or the Right, for anti-capitalism or capitalism, the problem finally becomes inescapable: social inflation must be reduced by reducing public sector demand. But ways of achieving this, and ways of reducing social costs, will differ fundamentally, according to whether they involve new forms of individual commodity consumption or, on the contrary, the search for collective answers to collective problems. We have reached another central issue of the crisis.

10. Reducing social costs: exit left

Unlike earlier economic development, advanced capitalism is no longer propelled by a spontaneous dynamic of demand, reliant on what marxists have always called 'basic needs': those whose non-satisfaction is synonymous with destitution.[17] Marx believed that once basic needs had been met, increasingly 'rich', 'historic needs' would arise. Their practically limitless growth, he thought, would result from the development of production itself, which, across the environment, the civilisation, the social relations it produces, 'not only creates an object for the subject, but also a subject for the object'.[18]

In actual fact this creation of a 'subject for the object', of a demand for supply, was not a spontaneous process. From the mid-1950s onwards, the centres of capitalism were faced with the necessity to *produce consumers for their commodities*, needs to match the most profitable products. Following its spontaneous, capitalist dynamic, production had ceased to correspond to preexisting needs: in as much as such needs persisted (notably in housing, sanitation and public health) their satisfaction was not profitable, or not sufficiently so, for capital. And, conversely, the most profitable products did not match unsatisfied needs: *these needs had to be created*. Thus it was necessary to establish the material environment (chiefly through extensive urbanisation) and social and cultural context which would foster them. As Jacques Attali has shown,[19] the development of certain infrastructures, along with the expansion of *education* and *medicalisation*, shared this function – the creation of needs, the 'production of demand'. Now 'demand production costs' (which Attali includes in 'organisation costs'),

> rise faster, by their very nature, than output . . . the time required to bear and raise children, to nurse and to cure, to integrate individuals into an urban surrounding or to transport and distribute goods, is almost irreducible . . . organisation costs then represent a growing share of value produced, lowering the disposable surplus and, consequently, investment.[20]

So it is clear that the problem of 'organisation costs' and how to reduce them is inseparable from that of the model of consumption and development. According to the model chosen, reducing social costs will generate either poverty or, on the contrary, more well-being for all.

1. Above all, the break with capitalism requires that social costs be seen as an integral part of production costs and taken into account when designing and pricing a product. What is required here is nothing less than the *socialisation of production decisions* and *social control* of production itself. For clearly any company, whoever owns it, will always try to maximise its profits by neglecting 'external' costs (infrastructures, servicing, pollution, damage and repair) which are not its liability. Keeping decisions about production, consumption and public expenditure separate will give rise to a tendency to maximise at every level: the creation of maximum individual needs, satisfied with maximum commodities, in turn giving rise to maximum social needs and expenditure. Internalising external production and consumption costs and trying to lower them presupposes that a greater share of production

is decided and done locally by its very consumers, so as to re-establish our unity as producers, consumers and citizens.

This unification is not possible everywhere, or with everything. The division of labour on the scale of vast areas and populations (countries or continents) and the resulting specialisation and technical concentration cannot be avoided – especially when a single, medium-sized unit of production can serve the specific needs of a whole country. This is the case, for example, with products like bearings, gaskets, meters, telecommunications equipment, light bulbs, microprocessors, glass, some chemicals and metals, etc., and with most of the machinery needed for their manufacture.[21]

But on the other hand production of most so-called consumer goods *can* be decentralised; decided, managed and performed on a regional and local scale by the consumers and users themselves, taking into account all the costs and advantages of different production and consumption choices.[22] The establishment of capillary networks of small and medium-sized enterprises – production co-operatives, craft co-operatives, under local or regional management – answerable to their own communities and required to adjust output and ways of operating according to the actual choices of local people, is helped enormously by micro-electronics, which makes small units competitive with big companies. Economies of scale no longer exist for the production of most consumer goods, and for some capital goods as well.[23] Maximum flow ceases to be the goal, and thus there is a break with capitalist logic. What is aimed at instead is maximum efficiency, that is, optimal satisfaction of needs and desires with the minimum expenditure of labour, capital and resources.

The expression of choice, and the corresponding adjustment of production, is best achieved (as Ralph Nader has clearly shown) by self-managed consumer co-operatives. A 500-member retail co-operative (500 being the optimal number, according to American experience) needs two hours of voluntary labour per member per month, plus a book-keeper and an administrator to ensure continuity. Consumption decisions are expressed by purchasing decisions, at quarterly general meetings. Thus there is a break with market economy logic, if not with market relations themselves.

The decline of commodity exchange will be encouraged by setting up 24-hour community workshops for autonomous production. We shall return to this point later.*

2. As we have seen already, rising social costs have a double source: the pursuit of individual solutions to collective problems and the reproduction of inequalities at ever-higher levels. Following an anti-capitalist logic, the stabilisation of social expenditure requires: firstly, the pursuit of collective solutions to collective problems and secondly, breaking away from the ideology of privilege.

The decline in our self-reliance has been a consequence and a condition of the spread of commercial services and commodities. Extensive urbanisation, curative medicine and schooling have all played a crucial role in 'learning to consume' and in the disappearance of all the popular know-how on which self-reliance was based: treating common complaints and illnesses, cooking, repairing our houses, furniture and tools, caring for babies, keeping fit, etc.

The school and the health system have devalued the know-how and culture of the people in favour of a veneration of expert professionals whose monopoly in selling authorised goods and services necessarily assumed a monopoly in knowledge. Alongside this destruction of popular culture, extensive urbanisation has torn apart the fabric of social bonds and solidarity, spreading market relations and commodities into what were once areas of free activity and mutual aid. The collapse of spontaneous networks of self-help, ties between generations, mutual aid among neighbours, etc., has intensified demand not only for private goods and services but also for social services, for health care, council housing, welfare benefits, policing, etc.

In terms of social cost, the cheapest solutions to collective problems are collective ones. Nordal Akerman[24] has provided us with concrete evidence on the possibilities for *a posteriori* densification of scattered housing estates and on the advantages this would bring for the inhabitants. Concerning transport, little more needs to be said, except to underline that what is essential is not to speed up transport between home and work but to bring the two together and as far as possible unite them in one community. This is a

---

* See thesis 24.

fundamental point if we are to overcome the separation of production and consumption, work and free time.

In the field of health, the anti-capitalist solution is not endless expansion of curative medicine's over-specialised staff and equipment but rather reduction of the causes of disease through public health and hygiene policies. For these causes are essentially social and can only be reduced by the collective action of those who endure them. As Bruno Jobert puts it: 'Opening health centres is not enough . . . What is needed is to give workers the technical means to analyse their own working conditions – following the example of Italian unions – and to organise a collective response to the dangers they face. The necessary information can be gathered via environmental health committees, so that local groups and communities can exercise greater collective control over their own living conditions.' In short, we need to 'invert the logic of institutionalised health care and turn passive recipients into active participants in the management of their own environment.'[25]

From a sociological viewpoint, the dynamic of inequality – the endless sequence of 'catching up' and 'progress' – has been a crucial source of growth. As soon as a particular product is generally obtainable, inequality is reproduced by supplying a 'better' one which only the privileged can afford. This in turn will devalue the obtainable product, render it obsolete, and define the 'poverty' of those who cannot afford the 'better' one. Thus the reproduction of inequality – poverty and privilege – at ever-higher levels is a necessary condition for the indefinite growth of demand.

This dynamic cannot be restricted to only specific types of product. It feeds on – and is fed by – an ideology of privilege in which what is good enough for everyone is not good enough for anyone. Individual pursuit of 'better' goods and services, out of general reach, is especially apparent in the field of medicine. The 'best' doctors, by definition, are the ones who can give access to rare skills and technology, sources of privilege for themselves and their patients. To expand, or even maintain, a practice, each doctor must be 'better' than the rest, must provide rare forms of treatment. And at the very top of this pyramid come the grand masters of medicine, renowned for their exceptional skills, their prodigious successes. While practitioners struggle to outbid each other, treatment costs rise dramatically: this is supply inflation, and medical hierarchies and competition are its fundamental source. In continually intensifying its own hierarchy, through spectacular treatment of extreme cases, the medical world also continues to reproduce inequalities in society as a whole, and thus demand for exceptional and more costly therapies.

The argument that medical 'progress' and the reduction of disease depend on this process had been refuted time and again. We need only point out that half of all medical expenditure goes on 4 per cent of the sick, with 40 per cent being spent on 1 per cent of patients. The majority (80 per cent) of patients account for only 20 per cent of expenditure. Essentially, 'medical advances' benefit only the tiny minority of patients who need dramatic, emergency treatments and who can thus add to the fame and status of those who develop and apply them. Meanwhile, prevention and treatment of the commonest ailments, whose social cost is greatest (respiratory tract diseases, rheumatism, flu, etc.) hardly progress at all. For these disorders, by virtue of being endemic and commonplace, can be treated only by methods that will also become commonplace, available to anybody. There is no scope for star turns: improved therapy will not be any famous physician's monopoly. The medical hierarchy, therefore, is not interested.

In conclusion, the level of health costs cannot be stabilised, let alone reduced, without egalitarian reorientation of medicine and, more generally, of public health policies. Reversing the present trend, this reorientation must prioritise improvements in standards of health for the general population over specialist treatment. It must institute standards of health care which are both effective and available to all, and which will improve *for everyone* when more efficacious, *generalisable* forms of treatment have been developed.

At present, it is the Scandinavian countries which have gone furthest in defining and applying this kind of general standard. There, the pursuit of better all-round health protection and more efficacious ways of combating the commonest diseases takes precedence over the heroic performances of intensive-care medicine. General availability, not monopoly and privilege, has become the criterion for the development of new techniques. 'What is good is good, what is enough is enough', could be the motto of this approach. 'More' and 'better' would equal luxury and waste, creating privilege for the few, frustration for the many.

But it is clear that the only general standard which everyone is likely to accept is one established *by* everyone – one which gives maximum scope for collective control of living conditions and health factors in communities and workplaces.

However, a general standard cannot be sought in just one area. It cannot be developed and accepted in the field of health unless it is similarly pursued in all areas of consumption, and defined through mass participation. Dissatisfaction, the endless search for 'more' and 'better', is not born of the autonomous awareness of lack or inadequacy but of the *existence* of supposed improvements which the market supplies to a minority. So collective control of supply, and thus of decisions about social production, is the key to an egalitarian transformation of the model of consumption and to a corresponding expansion of non-market, autonomous production.*

Collective control obviously means breaking with capitalist logic and capitalist ideology. It implies a social project which can oppose and reverse those forces that now operate 'spontaneously'. The choice here is a stark one, the alternatives sharply opposed. For if society does not use micro-electronics to extend the spheres of autonomy and self-management and thus to overcome the crisis by breaking with capitalism, then capitalism itself will 'spontaneously' turn towards a new form of industrialisation which (as we will see in the following section) will mark the final triumph of the reign of commodities.

11. Reducing social costs: exit right

According to marxist theory, as the market becomes saturated, capital meets increasing 'difficulties in realising surplus value': in other words, it becomes harder and harder to sell output at the usual price whereas sales costs keep rising steeply. During the last growth period, the difficulties of realising surplus value took on a distinctive new form: an increasing difficulty in producing the consumers for commodities coupled with the rising cost of what Jacques Attali calls 'production of demand'. 'Production of demand' had become heavily dependent on a system of services

---

* For a theoretical definition of the model of consumption, see theses 23–25 below.

(education, information, health care, urbanisation, transport, propaganda, etc.), whose productivity kept falling despite their rising cost. Following the rationale of capitalism, the cost of these services must be drastically cut if the crisis is to be overcome and a new accumulation cycle launched.

This is the role assigned to information technology. It is expected to reduce the costs of producing the appropriate consumers. It should furthermore make it possible to industrialise one-to-one services, namely those of physicians, psychologists, educators, etc.; to transfer the production of consumers to the consumers themselves – with the help of computer programs which will be sold to them with a sizeable profit. 'Autosurveillance society' is Jacques Attali's description of this autoproduction of consumers to the standard required by industry.[26] This auto-production must replace public services in two essential spheres – education and health. For it is there that staffing levels and social costs are highest, and the fall in productivity most severe.

Education, to a large extent, can be transferred to commercially manufactured teaching machines at every level: computer games and machines to teach walking, speech, singing, drawing, basic maths, etc.; auto-instruction programs for secondary and higher education; recycling programs for adult education – self-assessment of skills and knowledge in relation to changing social and professional standards.

In this way individuals will pay industry for the means (terminals, teletext receivers, access to memory storage and specific programs) of autoproduction, auto-integration and auto-surveillance – the means to ward off anxiety, isolation, fear of demotion, unemployment and marginalisation.

Health care will undergo a similar evolution. Consultation with a doctor, psychiatrist or sexologist is to be replaced by dialogue with a computer – for self-examination, self-diagnosis, self-treatment. The rate of medical insurance contributions and benefit entitlement will be made to depend on adhering to a computer-prescribed health regime adjusted to each individual's biological parameters. Check-up machines, computerised massage and gymnastics appliances, yoga and relaxation programs and videos, etc. – almost all one-to-one services can be industrialised and capitalised. Even 'sexual service' itself (that is, prostitution) can be, and is already, industrialised, with gadgets and visual material to aid masturbation or simulate intercourse: inflatable dolls, videos, etc.[27]

From the economic point of view, the effect of this industrialisation is to make 'productive' in the capitalist sense (productive of surplus value) those activities which formerly have been financed by taxes on potential profit or by 'unproductive' spending. What was once a *cost* is now a source of *profit*.

From the technical point of view, the specificity of this type of industrialisation is the non-material character of the commodities produced. For the material products (computer/telecommunications networks, terminals, storage units, tapes, etc.) are only *means of access* to a non-material commodity: 'information', whose production cost is negligible, exchange value (selling price) high and whose consumption and production can grow without generating external costs or running into the same physical limits (gluts, bottlenecks, pollution) as material production.

In terms of fundamental economic categories, this marks the extension of the sphere of capitalist production to encompass activities formerly belonging to the (re) production of the labour force. The cost of this (re)production (maintenance, training, socialisation, health care) is sharply reduced while part of the network of services previously paid for by social contributions or taxes is shifted on to the individual. Industrialising these services thus reduces compulsory deductions and increases individual purchases of new forms of commodities. It creates a new market. The outcome, then, is 'a fall in wage costs without a fall in consumption', 'a rise in profit without a drop in demand'. We have the basic characteristics of what Michel Aglietta[28] defines as 'neo-Fordism', a system whose meaning and methods Jacques Attali has interpreted with his concept of 'autosurveillance society'.[29]

Helped by the liberation of time, *capitalist* development of autoservices and a new type of autoproduction can thus turn the desire for autonomy and control of the social environment away from its original goal and incorporate it into commodity relations. The world of 'prosumption' described by Alvin Toffler[30] does not necessarily mean absolute self-determination by autonomous producers. Rather than being autonomous activities which extend individuals' and communities' spheres of control, autoproduction and autoservices can be centrally programmed through the information technology they use. Central programming of autosurveillance will use *radial* communications networks giving everyone individual access to a central memory, and will rule out both *transversal* communication – and thus free, individual exchange of experience and information – and collective access to memory stores and collectively run decision making processes. The power of systems (state, technical and commercial) over individuals is therefore reinforced, while the capacity of the periphery to react on the centre is eliminated.[31]

In this way, individuals can be made to train themselves, maintain themselves and 'produce' themselves to fit a social norm which is pre-programmed by the autoproduction technology that they use. The desire for autonomy and free time is exploited and turned against its subject. What should be the material basis for our control over our own lives serves instead to imprison us in solitary autoconsumption.

This capitalist 'way out' of the crisis, though certainly on the horizon, nevertheless brings changes which are irreconcilable with capitalism's own ideology and rationality. Automation of tertiary sector operations and non-material production is fundamentally unsuitable for creating sufficient demand for the bulk of commodities on the market. It rules out a new cycle of intensive accumulation and the kind of regulation by which economic growth maintains itself through the wages it distributes and wage-earners' consumption.

On the contrary, non-material output requires very little capital and very little labour. Thus only a very small proportion of the gains from its sale can be reinvested. Such gains will therefore be revenue rather than profit, and most of them will have to be consumed by the new ruling elites and redistributed to the population independently of any work performed. Only this redistribution can give individuals the means to consume what must be sold.

The provision of means of payment to enable people to consume particular commodities will mark the final triumph of the reign of commodities *and* the negation of commodity relations. For then consumption will no longer satisfy the human needs (or desires) which arise from and motivate the performance of work; it will satisfy instead the need of the economic system to supply the available commodities with appropriate consumers. And so the circle is closed: the boundary between production and consumption, people and commodities, gets blurred. Commodities produce the people who are needed to get commodities consumed and produced. Individuals, consumers themselves, become commodities, produced or self-produced and sold at a profit. (And this is not an entirely new phenomenon: the engineers of the soul already supply industry with the individual profile – tastes, values, views and outlook – matching the commodities which must be consumed.)

We will return later* to the kind of power structure required by this social order – a social order which Jacques Attali rightly sees as 'the supreme incarnation of the commodity system': where *commodities buy their consumers.*[32]

But such an outcome to the crisis is not inevitable – or at least not yet. There is an alternative: 'progressively reducing worktime and the size of the tools of production'; promoting 'technology which is "open", not restrictive and centralised'; encouraging 'use of free time for creativity not consumption',[33] for the contraction, not expansion, of market relations; using information technology *horizontally* so that people can control their own social co-operation, rather than *vertically* for centralised social control over people.

---

* See thesis 16, III.

III. Automation and the death of capital

12. The micro-electronic revolution

Unlike the mega-technologies of the industrialist era, which were an obstacle to decentralised, community-based development, automation is socially ambivalent. The mega-technologies were a one-way street, whereas micro-electronics is a crossroads: it neither excludes nor imposes a form of development. Nuclear energy or the space programme *can only* lead to hyper-centralisation, whereas micro-electronics can equally lead to self-management, or even to self-managed centralisation. However, it cannot, in any circumstances, lead to a new, long cycle of capitalist accumulation.

This has been soundly demonstrated by studies abroad, notably by Günter Friedrichs, head of the automation department of the West German metal-workers union (I.G. Metall). He has shown that robotics and office automation can replace traditional systems by equipment with a higher performance and a lower cost per unit of output.[1] They can achieve simultaneous savings in investment (constant fixed capital), labour (variable capital) and raw materials (constant circulating capital), especially energy. This is precisely why they are such a radical innovation, fully justifying the expression 'micro-electronic revolution'.

For the first time since the invention of the electric motor, productivity in sector one (production of means of production) is continuing to rise faster than in sector two (consumer goods): the first factories without workers are those where robots manufacture robots. The value of constant fixed capital per unit of output diminishes rapidly and the value of variable capital falls to that of maintenance work. In short, the technological revolution brings a transformation which completely overturns the bases of economic reasoning. Unlike previous technological revolutions it does not just bring down the value of fixed capital per unit of output; it sets up a decline in the *total mass* of fixed capital employed to produce a rapidly increasing volume of commodities.

When the state stimulates investment, it thus clearly stimulates the renewal of the means of production and the revival of the rate of profit, but also the destruction of capital (through company closures, scrapping of existing machinery) and jobs. According to research in West Germany,[2] DM 1,000 million invested in industrial plant would have generated two million jobs from 1955–60 and 400,000 jobs from 1960–65. From 1965–70 the same sum would have *destroyed* 100,000 jobs and from 1970–75 it would have *destroyed* 500,000. In France, the officially registered decline in the industrial workforce has been 53,000 jobs per year.

Thus the revival of investment cannot revive growth, at least while technological transformation is continuing. Another new cycle of growth based on automation depends on a cultural transformation which has hardly begun, and a fundamental change in economic systems themselves. Labour time can no longer be the measure of exchange value, nor exchange value the measure of economic value. Wages can no longer depend on the amount of work performed, nor the right to an income on having a job.

How we define these transformations and how we control them politically are the basic issues of the present crisis.

13. Impossible capitalism

This crisis is unique because the technological changes through which capitalism responds to it cannot be controlled within its own rational framework. While speeding up destruction of capital and jobs, these changes make possible the production of an increasing quantity of commodities with a rapidly falling amount of capital and labour. Of course, 'making more with less' has always been a maxim of political economy, but this goal has only been pursued from the point of view of *relative* magnitude (less capital and labour per unit of output) within the framework of a growth of *absolute* amounts (more capital made profitable by production growing faster than investment). Now, as we have seen, the effect of automation is to reduce the absolute amount of capital which can be valorised by the production of a growing amount of commodities, both material and non-material.

It is true, of course, that these reduced quantities of capital can be a lot more profitable than in the past. But it is precisely because they are so profitable that there is a problem. For in the fully automated factory, the quantity of living labour drops towards zero, and so does purchasing power distributed as wages. Automation abolishes workers: equally, it abolishes potential buyers. From now on, one of two things can happen:

1. The law of the market works effectively and the *relative prices* of automation's products fall sharply – towards a value equal to the maintenance, reproduction and operating costs of automated plant and equipment. The wage bill becomes negligible, the workforce tiny. Permanently employed workers become a narrow social stratum, alongside vast numbers of unemployed (30 to 50 per cent of the 'active' population).* Some of the latter swell the ranks of the 'new tertiary sector', where they are forced into desperate, frenetic competition to sell domestic or sexual services to the narrow stratum of well-paid workers and employers. We are left, then, with the sort of economy now predominant in parts of North and South America (New York, Brazil, Mexico, etc.) where pauperism and overabundance of commodity goods and services go hand in hand, where organised society marginalises and represses a dispossessed social majority: slum-dwellers in the shadows of skyscrapers precariously surviving on crime and the underground economy.

But, in spite of right-wing politicians like Thatcher and Reagan, this alternative is less likely than the following:

---

* It is not an exaggeration to predict unemployment rates of 30 to 50 per cent by the end of the century, as do American economists like Peter F. Drucker or Pat Choate. A decline of 20 to 30 per cent of the quantity of wage labour by the end of the century corresponds to a differential of only 1–1.5 per cent between the annual growth of productivity (presently 3 to 4 per cent overall) and the growth of GNP. Considering already existing rates of unemployment, a level of 30 to 50 per cent by the end of the century may seem a moderate prediction. Demographic growth and the increasing proportion of women seeking jobs may produce even higher levels in certain countries.

2. Monopolies and cartels prevent massive price-cutting, and the products of automation (like the sale of 'non-material goods') bring in huge profits. These profits, however, prove impossible to reinvest (that is, to accumulate as capital)[3] because production requires less and less capital and distributes very little in wages, and thus does not generate expanding effective demand. So a large proportion of profits will have to be redistributed to enable commodities to be purchased, and to prevent the economy from collapsing. Consumption henceforth turns into a sort of social duty on a par with remunerative work: it is seen as one factor in the maintenance of social order, integrating and normalising. Paid consumption of commodities is erected into a system of control. And it is towards this solution (to which we will return later) that we are now moving.

Confronted with a technological revolution which permits the production of a growing volume of commodities with diminishing quantities of labour and capital, the aims and methods of economic management clearly *cannot* remain those of capitalism, any more than social relations can remain based on the sale of labour power, that is, on waged work. But neither can this management be socialist, since the principle 'to each according to his labour' has become obsolete and the socialisation of the productive process (which, according to Marx, was to be completed by socialism) has already been accomplished. Automation, therefore, takes us *beyond capitalism and socialism*. And this is the central issue – what *kind* of 'beyond'? There are two basic alternatives: fully '*programmed*' (in Alain Touraine's sense of the word), technocratic societies, or a liberated society, which Marx called 'communist', in which the necessary production of necessities occupies only a small part of everyone's time and where (waged) *work* ceases to be the main activity.[4]

Of necessity, these two types of society both need to separate the right to an income from the possession of a job. Their differences are nonetheless fundamental.

14. The end of the society of work

The micro-electronic revolution heralds the abolition of work.

This abolition must be understood in a double sense:

a) the quantity of labour needed for most material production and organisational activities rapidly becomes marginal;
b) work no longer involves direct contact between worker and matter. The transformation of the latter ceases to be the result of direct, sovereign individual activity.

These developments, which most 'marxists' either ignore or blame on the perverse effects of capitalism, according to Marx actually signal its end, and the objective maturity of communism. Indeed, Marx forecast that the 'transformation of the means of labour into the automatic process' would go together with *'the abolition of direct individual labour and its transformation into social labour'*.[5] The socialisation of work thus eliminates the individual knowledge that goes with a skilled job to give work the character of 'directly social activity', in which individuals participate not as people with personal abilities but as social individuals with socially determined abilities. This evolution is now practically complete.[6]

As Marx foresaw, the nature of work (its 'determined character') has become irrelevant. We say 'I'm working' or 'I've got a job', not 'I'm working on this or that.' Work no longer involves the identification of an individual with an activity 'which determines him in his particular being', as in the days when we would say: 'This is my skill, my trade.' To work is just to do this or that, here or there . . . it hardly matters.[7]

This 'indifference to determined content', however, has not brought with it the identification of the individual with society – 'as if with his own organic body' – envisaged by Marx. Quite the contrary: it has led to disaffection from work in general. Work is now only a source of social identity and personal achievement for the rapidly dwindling minority of 'professionals' who one way or another keep exclusive rights to the know-how they personally exercise.

For example, in Sweden, according to polls the proportion of women and men for whom work is the most important part of their lives has fallen from 33 per cent in 1955 to 17 per cent in 1977. In West Germany, the proportion of people for whom free-time activity is more important than work rose from 36 per cent in 1962 to 56 per cent in 1976. An opinion poll in France in autumn 1981 put the following question to a sample of workers: 'If you had the choice, would you give up your job?' The responses confirmed that 'the more people earn, the more attached they are to their work' (but then we know income goes up according to workers' qualifications and personal responsibility): 61 per cent of those earning between 4,000–6,000 F per month replied affirmatively, against 34.5 per cent of those earning more than 10,000 F, the average being 44.9 per cent.[8]

Of all contemporary socio-cultural changes, this disaffection from work is the most significant. It is undermining the moral and ideological foundations of industrialism. Already apparent before the acute phase of the present crisis (of which it was a determining factor, as we have seen), it has spread even faster through reduction by automation of socially necessary work time. Which is why societies everywhere *are organising this reduction in ways which hide its reality.* But there can no longer be full-time waged work for all, and waged work cannot remain the centre of gravity or even the central activity in our lives. *Any politics which denies this, whatever its ideological pretensions, is a fraud.*

15. Labourist conservatism

The right to work, the right to a job and the right to an income have been confused for a long time. They cannot be confused any longer. Unemployment benefits and early retirement are an acknowledgement of this fact – but at the same time they conceal it. Paying the unemployed, in Northern European countries, 70 per cent of their former wage or pensioning-off workers over 55 (over 50 in some crisis-hit sectors) on 70–90 per cent of their wage amounts to a *de facto* recognition that the right to an income can no longer be made dependent on having a job.

But this recognition is at the same time denied. Treating unemployment as if it were an accidental, temporary phenomenon and paying benefit as a charity rather than a right avoids the fact that there cannot be full-time, full employment, now or in the future. Unemployment and the unemployed are treated as though full-time jobs were and should remain the rule and the norm: either you must work full time or, in return for benefit, you must be unemployed and abandon all activity, even unpaid.[9] The alternative of full-time work or total unemployment implicitly denies the reduction of socially necessary work time, while sharing out this reduction in the most unequal way: penalising and marginalising those who could have gained from it (the unemployed) in order to preserve the norm of full-time work and *through it, the social relations between employers and employees.*

These relations, based on the bosses' power over the workers, can survive only if work is the employees' main occupation. Their dependency on their employer then comes to dominate their lives – which are entirely organised and centred around work. But if, on the other hand, work took up only 30 hours or less per week, it would become just one activity among others which were equally important or even more important. The relation of existential submission to employers could hardly be kept up; the workforce would no longer passively accept the bosses' decisions or their power. This, then, is the fundamental aim of keeping full-time work as the norm – *to maintain the relations of domination based on the work ethic.*

This political preservation of the ideological bases of domination has a high social cost. It leads inevitably to a dualistic division of the active population: on one side, acting as the repository of industrialism's traditional values, an elite of permanent, secure, full-time workers, attached to their work and their social status; on the other, a mass of unemployed and precarious casual workers, without qualifications or status, performing menial tasks.

All industrial societies are moving towards this 'dualism' (which has always been conspicuous in Japan) in which the class of permanent workers is destined to play a conservative role as defender of the old order.[10] On the other hand, the mass of disaffected non-workers is the *possible* social subject of the struggle for work-sharing, generalised reduction of work time, gradual abolition of waged work by the expansion of autoproduction, and for a living income for all. The boundary between Left and Right now clearly extends *inside* the world of work – and in fact it always has.[11]

16. Living-dead capitalism

As automation rapidly cuts the number of permanent, full-time jobs, the labour elite's hegemony can be maintained only by more or less authoritarian methods, while social control of the rising mass of non-workers demands more or less specific policies. These can be summarised as follows:

1. **The regimentation and segregation** of non-workers has already begun. The scale of unemployment and the payment of non-workers are disguised by measures such as: a higher school-leaving age; paid training schemes and higher education courses clearly lacking career outlets; extended conscription; poorly paid, paramilitary 'work experience' schemes and 'youth opportunities' programmes (performing tasks which would be unprofitable if a free workforce were used); increased arms production; limited wars, etc.

Segregation of people for whom there is no permanent, full-time work is the common characteristic of all these measures. How authoritarian this segregation will be depends on the political form and traditions of individual regimes: apartheid, gulags, compulsory paramilitary service; shanty-towns and North American-style urban ghettos, crowding together people who are mostly unemployed; or gangs of unemployed youth, subsidised eternal students and endless apprenticeships, temporary, holiday and seasonal workers, etc.

In every case, the unemployed are *socially marginalised*, even when they are the majority (as in South Africa, or some North American cities). They are deemed to be socially inferior and inadequate and effectively denied all social participation and activity. They remain outcasts and objects of resentment, begrudged whatever charity society grants them. A stratification which repudiates equal rights and justifies itself through quasi-racist hatred and contempt – this is the price we pay for the preservation of the labour elite's hegemony.

2. **Dualistic stratification** of social activity is an organised, technocratic form of segregation.[12] It splits the population into members of two different sectors. The first, which is highly productive and internationally competitive, includes advanced industries and the services (transport, communications and distribution) which influence their costings. The second sector covers low-productivity occupations which have no effect on the

first sector's costs and do not need precise profit and productivity norms: personal care and services, handicrafts, entertainments, the leisure industry, etc.

The second sector (which the promoters of this concept derisively call 'convivial') is explicitly subordinate to the first, politically as well as economically and ideologically. The labour elite, with its productivism and work ethic, remains hegemonic. However small a minority, it constitutes the ruling class, allowing small businesses, services and commercial activities to proliferate in its shadow. These may be used as subcontractors (as in Japan and Italy) on jobs for which the first sector is too inflexible, too slow to adapt.

Yet this 'spatial' dualistic organisation, as Guy Aznar calls it,[13] can only be provisional and temporary. For in the first place the labour elite will tend to get smaller and smaller. As ever more people seek refuge in a more relaxed and more frugal way of life in the second sector, so the possible outlets for the first sector's products inevitably decline. And at the same time the proliferation of suppliers of personal care and services will clash with the trend towards industrialising/computerising non-material production. This latter can only be achieved by depriving more and more people in the second sector of their livelihoods – people who must then, one way or another, be guaranteed an income independent of any work.

3. **Autoproduction and autosurveillance.** For the ruling class, the problem is thus threefold:

a) How to create demand for industrial production of non-material goods;

b) How to provide occupations for the mass of people thrown out of work by automated and computerised production – occupations which do not compete with this form of production;

c) How to pay people for these occupations so as to make demand effective.

There can be only one solution: people must be paid to consume the products supplied. Consumption must be put on a par with work and must be rewarded accordingly. Individuals must be paid in relation to their consumption of non-material goods insofar as this consumption is also productive: they produce themselves to meet the requirements of the goods they consume. Commodities buy their consumers[14] so that the latter, by the very act of consumption, become what society needs them to be.

It is this solution which is about to be applied, first of all to the young and the elderly. As Jacques Attali puts it: 'Now that consumption of education and health care is recognised as socially useful work, payments to children and the elderly are no longer seen as a form of assistance.'[15]

The former are paid to consume tuition, courses and apprentice-ships and thus to produce themselves as 'normal' citizens, whose ideology and aspirations conform to society's requirements. Before long, these courses and apprenticeships are going to be available in the form of computerised self-education and self-training. Once children reach school age, the state will provide them with pocket-money so that they can consume 'normalising' computer games: games whose built-in rules are virtually impossible to break or challenge because there is no visible subject prescribing them against whom the child can rebel. The rules are part of the machine itself, part of the world of objects. Computer games give the ideological choices of their programmers the status of incontrovertible 'objective necessities'.

As for the elderly, they are paid to accept their exclusion from all social activity – on condition that they adopt 'a way of life which [taking into account individuals' constitutions and predis-positions] can minimise health costs.'

Being ill is then experienced as a weakness, a sin and a crime, for which we can only make amends by following the prescribed, optimal way of life, by consuming a perfect copy of ourselves . . . we incessantly compare ourselves with a sensible, acceptable mirror-image, an image which increas-ingly becomes a single, standardised model to be imitated.[16]

We are constantly presented with detailed breakdowns of the causes of death, with the basic parameters of the model, with calculations of the social and individual cost of abnormal behaviour . . . Economic policy no longer consists of managing large-scale social expenditure . . . but of the explicit production of behavioral norms for all economic agents regulated by variations in insurance contributions or penalties: the capitalist state buys individual conformity to the norm, pays individuals to consume the model, and thus creates demand.[17]

This social model can be developed into further spheres of normalisation.[18] But, while Jacques Attali presents it as the solution to the crisis which capitalism is adopting, in reality it has only a *formal* resemblance to capitalism. The remuneration of citizens assumes the *semblance* of the wage, products consumed assume the *semblance* of commodities, and social relations the *semblance* of market relations; but these are hollow appearances. What is being preserved *is not the capitalist system but capitalism's system of domination, whose chief instruments were the wage and the market.* For now the goal of production is not and cannot be capital accumulation and valorisation.[19] Its primary objective is control and domination. Products are no longer supplied to maximise flow and profit – an idea which loses its meaning in a society where consumers are paid to consume and producers are a minority – but to maximise control and manipulation. Essentially, they become instruments of control in the hands of a ruling class whose power no longer rests on property but on controlling the system of control. Production system and control system become one and the same.[20] We are much closer to a totalitarian society run by a technocracy with a quasi-military hierarchy than to bourgeois capitalist society. Alain Touraine's definition of technocracy perfectly fits this society, which keeps the semblance of capitalism while losing the substance: domination by a technical system which has no purpose, whose managers are its servants not its masters.[21]

Whether this technocratic domination is (or will be) of the Left or the Right is a secondary question. What is at stake is the technocracy itself: whether it will be strengthened or eliminated.

IV. A way out of capitalism

17. The concept of an income for life: the '20,000 hours'.

In itself, the right to an income independent of a job is thus no guarantee of freedom, equality and security. It can be easily accommodated within an elitist technocracy and/or a system of totalitarian control reaching into our intimate relation with ourselves.

The abolition of work alone is not liberation. Liberty, by its very essence, cannot come from a technological change: it cannot be the effect of which technology is the cause. Technology can only create new material conditions. Those created by automation will encourage or jeopardise our personal development according to the social and political project underpinning their implementation. The guarantee of an income independent of a job will only bring freedom if it is accompanied by *the right to work for everyone*; that is, the right to participate in the production of society, in the creation of socially desirable wealth, the right freely to co-operate with others in the pursuit of our own goals.

The guarantee of an income independent of a job will be emancipatory or repressive, from the Left or the Right, according to whether it opens up new spaces for individual *and social* activity or whether, on the contrary, it is only the social wage for compulsory passivity.

The concept of a guaranteed income for life has its supporters on the Right as well as the Left. It is as old as the industrial revolution itself, having been put into practice, following the Speenhamland decision of 1795 and the Poor Laws, in a form which, through its unintended consequences, led to its abandonment. The concept was taken up again in various forms, in Britain, particularly in the twenties and thirties, by the Social Credit Movement,[1] later, in the United States during the Nixon administration, by senators Humphrey and Hawkins, whose legislative proposals were defeated by a narrow margin.[2]

As seen by its conservative advocates (among them Milton Friedman), a guaranteed minimum income for life and its distribution in the form of negative income tax above all offers the advantage of simplifying government. Negative income tax allows the abolition of a complex variety of benefits and allowances each requiring separate administration (housing benefit, family allowances, maternity benefit, basic pensions, supplementary and unemployment benefit, etc.) and their replacement by a single system: above a certain income, you pay tax to the Inland Revenue; below it, they pay you. This system can bring substantial savings insofar as it cuts off benefits and allowances to households whose resources take them above the threshold. Thus, in its conservative variant, a guaranteed income has the essential aim not of eradicating poverty and unemployment, but of making them socially acceptable at the least cost to society. Dualistic social stratification is therefore inevitably maintained, and even reinforced.

In its left-wing form, a guaranteed income independent of a job follows a radically different logic. It is not seen as a wage for unemployment, nor as charity for women and men marginalised by society. Instead, it becomes the right of each citizen to receive – *distributed throughout their life* – the product of the minimum amount of socially necessary labour which s/he has to provide in a lifetime.

This amount is unlikely to exceed 20,000 hours in a lifetime by the end of the century;[3] it would be much less in an egalitarian society opting for a less competitive, more relaxed way of life.[4] Twenty thousand hours per lifetime represents 10 years' full-time work, or 20 years' part-time work, or – a more likely choice – 40 years of intermittent work, part-time alternating with periods for holidays, or for unpaid autonomous activity, community work, etc.

In the following paragraphs I will discuss the technical problems and ideological objections raised by this flexible distribution of a quantity of labour over an extended period. For now, what is important is the fact that socially useful work will no longer be anyone's full-time occupation, nor the centre of their life. Life, like society itself, will become multi-centred. A wide range of forms of production and of rhythms and styles of life will co-exist, each person moving in several different spheres and finding their own balance in the passage from one to the other. Waged work will cease to be the primary activity but, through the guaranteed income for life which it provides for all, it will remain the economic basis for a limitless variety of possible activities without economic objectives or economic logic. We will return to this later.

18. Towards the abolition of wage labour: the social income

From this perspective, and in keeping with the socialist movement's original vision, the guarantee of an income for life is no longer seen as a compensation or allowance, or an extension of individual dependency on the state, but as *the social form which income takes* when automation has abolished, along with a permanent obligation to work, the law of value and wage labour itself. Necessary production requires such a small quantity of labour that no one could survive if they were paid only for the hours they actually worked. And inversely, the increasing output achieved with falling labour costs can only be distributed if it gives rise to the creation and distribution of means of payment corresponding to its own volume and not to the value of labour expended.[5]

Guaranteed income thus cannot be based on the 'value' of labour (that is, on what the social individual must consume in order to reproduce the labour power which s/he has expended doing waged work), nor seen as a reward for effort. Its essential function is to distribute to everyone the wealth created by society's productive forces *as a whole* and not by the sum of individual labours. We have then, following Marx's formula in 'Critique of the Gotha Programme', gone beyond the principle of 'to each according to his labour'; the principle 'to each according to his needs' must now regulate production and exchange.[6] The terms 'social wage', 'social dividend' and 'social income' – which we will retain here – are all equally appropriate to describe everyone's right of access to the social wealth which they have combined to produce through their intermittent work.[7]

Payment of a 'social income' to meet the needs of the *citizen* rather than the *worker* is already anticipated in certain union agreements or institutions which, potentially, open on to a post-capitalist, post-socialist logic. The Swedish economist Gösta Rehn[8] pioneered a definition of labour time measured over a lifetime, which would enable anyone, at any age, to take an advance on their retirement pension, as long as certain quotas were met. Rehn's proposal was refined, and in some aspects reversed, by Gunnar Adler-Karlsson.[9] If, for Rehn, everyone is born with a specific capital of time on which they may draw throughout their life, for Adler-Karlsson, we are born with a debt to society which we will repay in working hours in the course of our lives, when we choose, provided again that certain quotas are met. In return society will guarantee us an income for life. Of course anyone will be free to work more and thus earn more than their total debt. Or alternatively we can choose to earn only what we owe, by working the minimum number of hours per year to guarantee an income. The possibilities are numerous – lending or borrowing hours to or from society, repaying in advance or contracting an extra debt. Depending on circumstances and society's needs, citizens will be encouraged to lend or to borrow work time.

The anticyclical role which this lending and borrowing can play is central to Rehn's proposal; Adler-Karlsson, a more radical innovator, is concerned instead with giving everyone a permanent choice between different ways of life. The need for money or for time, the importance given to waged work or to free-time activity, can indeed vary drastically in the same person according to their age, the number and ages of their children, encounters and discoveries that come early or late, etc.

Yet the break with the law of value – and with productivist logic, be it capitalist or socialist – is not explicit in the work of either writer. For them, a guaranteed income for life is really a deferred wage or an advance on a future wage, rather than a social income. And to pay for it they seem to envisage the same mechanisms which apply to pension funds and sickness or unemployment benefit: contributions or taxes deducted from wages and redistributed to workers who, temporarily or permanently, have ceased employment.

Implicitly, such a conception is still based on payment for work. The deferred or advanced wage received in periods of non-work is seen as something saved from previous earnings or borrowed from future ones. Even when they are not working, people are paid as workers, not as citizens.

There is a fundamental drawback to all this: by its ideological bias it stops us thinking through the logical consequences of the abolition of work. For as labour time drops, per year and per lifetime, the sum of contributions and taxes needed to pay for non-work will outstrip the yield of direct wages. Finally, the payment for non-work time will exceed payment for work. And so it becomes impossible to argue that the former should be deducted from the latter. What is being undermined is really the basic premise of industrial capitalism itself. This premise – on which the concept of 'value' is based and which gives rise to the 'law of value' that, for Marx, was the cornerstone of capitalist reasoning – is that the wage pays for *labour* to meet the *needs* which labour generates in those who supply it. But in fact it is no longer work and workers that must be paid, but life and citizens. Since people's labour is ceasing to be the main source of wealth, their needs can only be realised and products distributed if the means of payment are unrelated to the amount of labour required by production.

The abolition of wage labour, of market mechanisms and labour value, are necessary consequences of automated production and are also implicit in notions of work measured over a lifetime and a guaranteed income for life. When essential social production is realised not by individual labour but by the power of the agencies set in motion, agencies whose effectiveness is out of all proportion to the direct labour time spent in their production,[10] the 'right to work' can no longer be confused with the right to a paid job. Instead, citizens must, on the one hand, have the right to an income for life representing their share of socially produced wealth and, on the other, have the right of access by means of producing and creating goods which cannot be socially programmed, goods that they want to use, consume and exchange outside the market, in communities and local co-operatives. This is the realm of autonomous activity. We will return to this later.

19. Towards a social income

In practical terms, financing incomes for life does not raise any new problems, nor does it presuppose reinforcing the centralised state. It can best be accomplished by taxing automated production.

In 1983, Japanese employers proposed that robots should pay union dues. It would make much more sense if they were to pay social contributions, per unit of output, varied like VAT according to the model of consumption which is to be promoted.

This kind of variable taxation will thus have a double role. Firstly it will supply the fund from which to pay guaranteed incomes. And secondly it will prevent falling *relative prices* of those material and non-material goods whose production can be automated most rapidly, but whose endlessly rising consumption is not socially useful, desirable or even possible.

As the cost price of automated production drops, its taxation will thus replace market prices with a system of *political* pricing. What is involved here is nothing more than an extension of current practice in modern economies which all adjust the market price system by raising specific taxes (on alcohol, tobacco, petrol, cars, etc.) and giving out specific subsidies (to public services, agriculture, the arts, etc.). When automated production's cost price becomes negligible, and its market exchange value threatens to collapse, society has no choice but to adopt a system of political pricing reflecting its choices and priorities in individual and collective consumption. The disappearance of market laws (as Marx showed in the *Grundrisse*), just like the disappearance of the law of value, is an inevitable consequence of automation. Better then to break openly from capitalism, rather than shore up its facade through all kinds of subterfuge.

At the strategic level of social struggles, the transition to a post-capitalist economy is more or less anticipated in those union agreements which ensure that the increase in labour productivity will bring about a corresponding reduction of hours without any reduction of wages. To put it another way, *work which is eliminated is paid for in the same way as work which is performed*, non-workers paid in the same way as workers. The connection between pay and work performed is broken. That is the basic content of agreements which APEX has signed in Britain in the electronics industry, and of the agreement reached by New York dockers. This latter guarantees job security by sharing necessary work among the total number of dockers: as labour requirements fall, work time is reduced, but wages can never fall below the earnings of a 30-hour week.

Yet, as I have shown elsewhere,[11] agreements like this cannot be generalised under capitalism. They cannot be extended to the entire population simply through a series of union struggles and sectoral deals – even though these remain a precondition. For improvements in productivity differ widely from sector to sector, even from company to company. Indexation of work time according to its productivity (with wages kept constant) would lead to serious disparities which, if staffing levels in each sector are frozen, would lead to gross corporate privileges.

Moreover, productivity does not increase spontaneously: it is always a response to external constraints. Its increase does not automatically reduce working hours or bring about new forms of work-sharing; it will only do so if that is its goal, and if it is accompanied by new work patterns and flexible schedules.[12] Thus productivity growth can in no way be seen as an independent variable dictating the evolution of work time and staffing levels. On the contrary, it is the redistribution of work and reduction of hours that need to be planned in advance as independent variable and social constraints. As long as the planned goals are based on a realistic assessment of increases in productivity which can be achieved, the organisation of production will adjust to this external constraint, just as it has adjusted to Sunday rest, the banning of child labour, union rights, sick pay, etc., which were all considered unattainable at first.

Above all, then, generalised reduction of work time with guaranteed income presupposes a will to transform society – through new policies of time and employment, but also through union action and collective planning. Specifically, it will require centres for forecasting, planning and information-gathering; continual transfer of labour from rapidly automating activities to those where automation is slow; a labour exchange open to everyone, for jobs offered and wanted, where jobs can also be swapped or shared with others; polyvalent skills and high job mobility, with 'workers' able to move easily from highly automated occupations to more conventional ones – or even to do different jobs at different times of the year. Indifference to the content and nature of work here reacquires the positive meaning which Marx gave it in the *Grundrisse*. Only a society in which everyone possesses polyvalent, wide-ranging, interchangeable social skills can share out the greatest number of tasks among the greatest number of people, tasks which are themselves standardised, simplified and interchangeable.

20. Standardised work, shared work

Standardisation and simplification of skills – the effect of socialisation of the productive process – is the condition for permanent distribution and redistribution of socially necessary work among the greatest number of people, so that everyone can work and everyone can work less and less, as technology becomes more efficient. At a time when technology is rapidly and drastically reducing the quantity of necessary work, standardisation of work takes on a growing urgency. Indeed only this can prevent a minority of professionals monopolising the dwindling number of available jobs, establishing themselves as a technocratic caste and condemning the majority of the population to marginality and dependency.

Expecting automation to restore the skills which Fordism eliminated reveals a dangerous misconception. Were such a restoration possible, every type of job would demand skilled workers who had undergone lengthy and highly specialised training. It would therefore rule out the distribution and redistribution of a diminishing amount of work among as many people as possible. And thus it would tend to concentrate jobs and power in the hands of what I have called the labour elite, and to consolidate dualistic social stratification.

Automation and computerisation can be emancipatory only if they standardise and simplify even more tasks and functions than in the past – if, in other words, they enable everyone, after a universal basic training, to acquire a wide, adaptable range of qualifications, independently and swiftly. Only then can work which is reduced for all and shared by all become a right for all: the right to make and feel ourselves useful to society.

Computerisation can allow this standardisation of skills, this universal polyvalence. It *can* widen the area of self-management and democratic control – provided, of course, that it is made to serve these purposes.

Standardisation and simplification of work nevertheless raise two connected questions: whether heteronomous work can be acceptable, and whether highly qualified professionals can work short hours like anyone else. However, these questions are going to arise in new terms. We will return to them in thesis 23. The interaction of the spheres of heteronomous work and autonomous activity will be the subject of thesis 25.

21. Critique of market relations

In the preceding theses I have shown that the massive reduction of work time is *possible* by virtue of automation and *necessary* so that everyone can work – less and better. In this thesis and the one which follows, I intend to show that what is possible and necessary is also *desirable*; that the abolition of heteronomous waged work as a central activity is a condition (a necessary condition but not a sufficient one) for liberating and enriching all our lives. In so doing, I will be reaffirming the original aspiration of the workers' movement – in which the refusal of capitalism, the refusal of compulsory waged work and the refusal of domination are one and the same.

Beyond waged work, what is being challenged here is the primacy of the economic, that sphere in which every action is solely determined by the principle of *equal exchange*, where nothing has its own value, nothing is an end in itself. It is because capitalism reduces everything to economic categories that it is anti-humanist. This was how it was perceived by the early workers' movement, and this was what they fought against. The most fundamental and radical workers' demands were attacks on economic logic, on the utilitarian, exchangeist, quantitative conception of work and wealth.

Non-economic activities are the very fabric of life itself. They encompass everything which is done, not for money, but out of friendship, love, compassion, concern; or for the satisfaction, pleasure and joy derived from the activities themselves and from their end results.

In all pre-capitalist societies, these pleasurable activities were embedded into productive work. Work was given its rhythm by festivals and celebrations, with their songs and dances; the tools themselves were beautifully decorated . . . There was, in short, a genuine 'popular art' which integrated work and life to create a way of living that had meaning and value. This is not to deny that conditions were harsh, privations frequent and survival precarious, nor to deny that power was exercised oppressively, cruelly and despotically. It is simply to demonstrate that working was *also* a way of *being in the present*, of relating to others and to the world; that there was no separation between work, culture and life.

Moreover, social and personal relations were not dominated by market relations. They were governed by non-economic, non-monetary exchange – and in particular, formally or informally, by solidarity and mutual aid – by relationships which, however debased, were founded on giving and generosity, the original form (in ontological, not historical, terms) of the recognition of the other as another self.

The desire to 'make someone happy', to help others, to give without looking for anything in return, this is the very essence of love, of tenderness, affection, friendship and solidarity, of all relationships with others which enrich existence. Without it, life loses all meaning, is 'not worth living'.

It is industrialisation which has made work into a purely functional activity, separated from life, severed from culture, torn out of the fabric of human existence. No longer is work a way of living and acting together, no longer is the workplace a place of life, work time a reflection of seasonal and biological rhythms. Money, in the form of profits or wages, is the overriding goal of every activity, rather than pleasure and satisfaction. The triumph of market relations over relations of reciprocity, of exchange value over use value, has impoverished our lives and abilities.

Of course, there is no *a priori* reason why friendship, creativity, comradeship, generosity and festivity should not be given a place *within* heternonomous work. But the fact remains that they have been forcibly excluded from it, and that there is now neither time nor place for workers to share non-economic and non-market values and relationships, to bring together work, life and culture. And if workers lack that experience even outside work, it is hard to see how they would struggle to incorporate non-economic values within it. As long as working life, governed by the wage relation and the productivist logic of 'you're not here to enjoy yourself', fill the best part of our time, and the tyranny of the stop-watch divides working and living, we are equally unlikely to discover or re-invent non-economic wealth *outside* work. Only one thing could change this situation – a huge reduction of work time, accompanied by new policies on space and time, on urbanism, resources and culture.[13]

Reduction of work time and simultaneous expansion of the sphere of autonomous activity and non-market relations are prerequisites for transforming the physical conditions, atmosphere and lived experience of heteronomous work. Only then will its oppressive characteristics become unacceptable.[14]

But we must not expect that heteronomous work – work whose form and objectives are externally determined by the organisation of production on a national or continental scale – can ever be totally abolished or transformed into autonomous activity.

22. Critique of heteronomous work

Material constraints

The heteronomy of work is not just a consequence of capitalist organisation and division. At a deeper level, it is the result of division and organisation of production over vast economic zones, of mechanisation and interdependence. It should not be confused with the oppressive hierarchies and productive imperative generated by capitalism.[15] And it will not and cannot be eliminated by self-management or by the re-skilling and enrichment of work that self-management will foster at factory and shop level.

Heteronomous work is the inevitable outcome of socialisation of the productive process, itself made necessary by the quantity and diversity of knowledge and techniques which go into individual products. The production of an appliance as commonplace as a washing-machine, for example, brings together skills which far exceed the individual capacities of tens of thousands of people. The machine's components – stainless-steel drum, cast-iron frame, enamelled panels, electric circuits and motors, automatic control, rubber belts and piping, etc. – depend on very different industries and technologies. These in turn use machines (for laminating, smelting, wiredrawing, stamping, enamelling, coiling) whose design and construction presuppose a range of other industries and skills. Still further along the chain, the teaching, classification and development of these skills, the extraction of raw materials, transport of semi-manufactured products, etc., all rely on a complex network of institutions and services, and thus on a highly diversified society and its division into specialised agencies.

The co-ordination of a vast number of specialised tasks demands pre-established rules and procedures, leaving no room for individual improvisation or inventiveness. The social productive system can only operate like a single, giant machine, to which all the separate activities must be subservient. This subservience (in the mechanical, not the moral, sense) implies universal observation of the rules, and application of standards to ensure both the complementarity of the various products combined in general production and the interchangeability of similar products and services, whatever their origin.

Thus all work performed within social production is necessarily heteronomous: whatever level of skill is required, its form and content are determined by technical imperatives independent of all individual choice and interpretation; these imperatives severely limit the scope for individual judgement and initiative. This does not mean that heteronomy necessarily implies oppression and domination, boredom and/or exploitation. But it does necessarily imply the absence of individual control over the kinds of skill required and the overall purpose of collective work, and thus a degree of alienation.[16]

The limits of self-management

Heteronomous work can still be interesting. Making joints, bearings or microcircuits in a medium-sized factory meeting the needs of half of Europe can be, or can become, a skilled, interesting and pleasant activity, allowing a significant degree of autonomy in work relations at shop level, in timetabling, in adjusting to pre-established rules and standards. Heteronomy does not mean that the workplace has to be a hell or a purgatory. But it does mean that the purpose of production is beyond the control of individuals (why manufacture these particular gaskets, bearings, etc?) who have only an extremely abstract understanding of their task: the social machine has to be kept going, the 'Plan' has to be fulfilled. The influence that workers in any one production unit can have on the 'Plan' is inevitably slight, and does not extend beyond the conception stage.

For all these reasons, heteronomous work is impoverishing for those who are obliged to make it their permanent, full-time occupation. The level of skill involved makes no difference. Indeed, there are very few socially determined activities where increasing skill is not accompanied by ever-narrowing specialisations. A building labourer, for example, has a far greater range of abilities than an engineer specialising in pre-stressed concrete, or a microsurgeon. Research and development of fragmentation bombs or automatic weapons systems demands enormous skill and raises all kinds of absorbing scientific problems: that does not make it any less morally crippling.

The success of workers' struggles for self-determination of working conditions and self-management of the technical production process must not therefore be confused with the elimination of heteronomous work's inherent alienation. Oppressive hierarchies, laboriousness, monotony, boredom – all these can be eradicated, and the workplace can become a place of mutual exchange, co-operation and harmony. But such a liberation of *work relations* is not the same as autonomy of work itself or workers' self-determination (or self-management) of its overall purpose and content.

The possibilities for achieving excellent work relations and a congenial atmosphere are just the same whether one is producing chemical weapons or medicines, 'Action Man' or 'educational' games, pornography or art books. There can be no liberation without the liberation of *work relations*; nevertheless, the latter does not give everyone the ability to control the final results of the collective work in which they participate. Social collaboration on a regional or world scale cannot be self-determined or voluntary. Marx's 'productive collective worker' is as much an abstraction for each individual worker as an army's movements are to an ordinary soldier.

This is why the forms and content of socially determined work can only be ends in themselves in very exceptional circumstances. Those who want such work to be our reason for living and primary source of identity are justifying in advance all politics whose only goal is to keep people busy at any price – if need be by regimentation or wastage, by militarisation or by war itself.

To go beyond capitalism is, essentially, to go beyond a system of production for production's sake, towards a society where use values supersede exchange values and, consequently, economics does not determine and dominate social relations but rather is limited by and subordinate to the expansion of social relations of 'voluntary co-operation'.[17] In other words, to go beyond capitalism we must, above all, end the supremacy of commodity relations – including sale of labour – by prioritising voluntary exchange and activities which are ends in themselves.

Reduction of work time has nothing to do with emancipation if it merely leads to more time being spent on material and non-material consumption. It can be an emancipatory project only if combined with contraction of economic and market activity and expansion of activities performed for their own sake – for love, pleasure or satisfaction, following personal passions, preferences and vocations.[18]

But this sphere of autonomy cannot be all there is: it can only exist, and acquire value and substance, against a background of work that is both necessary and necessarily heteronomous (what Marx called 'the sphere of necessity'). I have already shown that complete elimination of this sphere is not possible. Nor is it desirable, as we will now see.

23.1 Demand for work – demand for society

A job which takes up less than 1,000 hours per year no longer has the same nature or meaning as one lasting 40 hours or more a week, year in year out. To be 'obliged' to work about 1,000 hours a year means you work two and a half days a week, or two weeks a month, or five months in a year; it means you can share a job with someone else, combine or alternate several occupations, mix heteronomous work with freely chosen activity, and so on.

However standardised, simple to learn or interchangeable, a job taking up less than 1,000 hours per year – and *a fortiori* several jobs totalling less than 1,000 hours – ceases to be a tiring, obsessive obligation, grinding you down and wearing you out; instead it is an occupation which is welcome for the diversity, contacts, rhythm and timing it adds to your life. As the time to be organised and filled in one's own way grows in importance, so standardised, heteronomous work will become all the more acceptable and attractive.

So there are no grounds for the objection that: 'when people are

guaranteed an income for life they will not want to work at all'.*
On the contrary, there is every reason to suppose that abolition of
the *permanent* compulsion to work, along with the development of
family, community, collective and co-operative life and activity,
will encourage people to seek socially determined work for the
same reasons as 'housebound women', retired people, the
unemployed and sons and daughters of peasants seek waged work,
however unrewarding. It provides an escape from the narrowness
and stifling conformity of the domestic unit or village community,
a way of meeting other people from other places with whom
relationships can be freer, less familiar, than with those who see
you first and foremost as daughter or daughter-in-law, sister or
cousin, and tie you to a carefully regulated world where everyone
must keep to their allotted place.[19] It allows you to feel useful to
society in a general sense, rather than in a particular way subject to
particular relationships, and thus to exist as a fully social
individual protected from the pressures of particular groups by
anonymous membership of society at large.

Thus, the more individual activity can blossom, and communities
of life and work be re-established, the more abstract and
heteronomous waged work will become appealing because of the
small emotional investment it requires. So we can predict that the
demand for abstract work will grow apace with the reduction of
obligatory work time, and will easily balance out the vacancies
generated by all those who want to give up their waged work
temporarily.

The supply and demand of jobs can then easily be adjusted by
having local, regional and national labour exchanges where those
wanting to leave a job will advertise its availability, only staying
on, if need be, until the arrival and induction of their successor, or
until s/he is accepted by their workmates. The mobility of the
workforce, the flexibility of hours and the working week, need not
be obstacles to continuity, professional integrity or team self-
organisation. It may even be possible for people who get to enjoy

---

*This objection is particularly common among those in the traditional Left who
still believe in the religion of work and in waged work as a source of identity and
personal achievement. Yet is is clearly paradoxical to glorify work like this while
believing that no one would want to work if they were not permanently forced to
do so.

working together as a team to move from heteronomous to autonomous, autoproductive activities and to change over from one sector, town or factory to another without splitting up.

23.2 Professionalism

For the most highly qualified activities there have always been more candidates than jobs available. The number of surgeons, therapists, engineers, researchers, musicians, journalists, etc., is restricted not by a scarcity of talent but because places are jealously guarded by professionals anxious to retain their monopoly or are awarded through competitive exams on a restricted-entry basis. Contrary to the myth, the good surgeon, the good researcher, administrator or journalist does not to need to work 14 hours a day monopolising several jobs in order to stay 'on form' and avoid being left behind. Quite the opposite – in all skills which bring together wide-ranging, constantly updated knowledge, great dexterity and intense concentration, the quality of work benefits from a reduction of its quantity. Taking time out to read, browse, reflect and diversify one's centres of interest stimulates imagination and creativity far more than constant pressure. Top-level research scientists, who are no longer forced to work fixed hours, prove the point, as do the growing number of doctors, consultant engineers and senior managers who have opted for job-sharing.[20]

A drastic reduction of work time in the most highly skilled professions will be all the easier to achieve as the freeing of time and provision of guaranteed incomes allows everyone who so desires to acquire those advanced skills where personal talent and expertise are irreplaceable and where productivity rises very slowly. The number of people with diverse and highly developed skills will thus tend to increase along with the automation of standardisable jobs.

The jobs now monopolised by a technocratic elite may therefore be shared out among a larger proportion of the population and cease to be the exclusive preserve of a caste. The power and privileges attached to them will thus tend to disappear. Those who perform such jobs will be – as is already the case in some kibbutzim – members of the community just like anyone else, dividing their time between professional work, autonomous activity and general tasks, no longer agonising day and night over power struggles, their 'career' and their social status.*

24. The necessary and the optional

Autonomous activity will not have the same meaning or function for those living in a rural society with a predominantly village-based economy as for those in an industrialised and urbanised society.

In the former, the bulk of necessities are locally produced, and self-consumption of local produce far exceeds commodity production and consumption. Industry only supplies additional products which, if need be, the village community can do without – above all, more efficient tools than the local workshop can manufacture. These facilitate local autoproduction, saving time and effort.

In this case, then, autoproduction, however much it may be formally autonomous or self-determined, is an activity which is *necessary* for subsistence. Choice can be exercised only over details, within narrow limits: you can decide to grow more potatoes than artichokes, more chick-peas than beans, to start the day half an hour earlier and have a longer siesta, etc., but the work still has to be done, as an imperative. Your subsistence depends on it. *It belongs to the sphere of necessity.*

On the other hand, industrial tools, produced by the heteronomous labour of waged workers, seem like a luxury: they are not absolutely indispensable but they are desirable, because they allow you to produce a little extra over and above what is necessary, while increasing your free time. Thus industrial production – as long as it stays within certain limits – is the precondition for the villager's real autonomy: the space to do what is not absolutely necessary, or the space to do nothing, to dream in the shade.

Here, then, the relation between the respective values (in the cultural and ethical sense) of industrial and domestic production is the reverse of that in industrialised societies. The existence of a space for autonomy (so restricted that we cannot call it a 'sphere')

---

* On the necessity of professionals and the non-necessity of their powers and privileges, see 'Individual, society, state' below.

depends on the products of heteronomous work. It is not something pre-given for a villager whose only activity is auto-production. For the villager, it may be even narrower than for a labourer doing a 60-hour week of heteronomous work.

In industrialised societies, on the contrary, self-determined activities only constitute a sphere of autonomy to the extent that what is necessary is guaranteed by heteronomous waged work. The mother who finishes her day at the factory only to rush off and collect her children, cook a meal and do the washing remains in the sphere of necessity even in her formally autonomous activity. When her work time *and her wages* are cut so that she has to spend three hours after work producing for herself and her family what two hours' wages would have bought her, then reduction of her heteronomous work does not enlarge her space of autonomy. When, on the other hand, she gets enough wages to pay for necessities *and* has a shorter working day, her disposable time increases together with her space of autonomy. The same is true when her time spent in waged work and therefore her wages are reduced, but, in the freed time, she is able to produce more use value or change than could be bought with extra wages.

So when I ascribed to heteronomous work the function of producing what is necessary and equated the sphere of necessity with the sphere of heteronomy (in theses 17 to 19 above, and in an earlier work),[21] it was not for arbitrary or ideological reasons. It was because it is in this way, and this way only, that the problem poses itself: almost everyone in industrialised societies purchases almost everything that is necessary (and many things which are not necessary) with the wages from heteronomous work. Under these conditions, freeing time will create new spaces of autonomy only if the time released does not have to be spent in the autoproduction of some of those necessities which previously could be bought. Reducing heteronomous work does not free time unless everyone is free to use this time as they choose. Necessities must be provided for by another source. Free-time activities, insofar as they are productive, will be concerned with autoproduction of all that is optional, gratuitous, superfluous, of all, in short, which is not necessary, which gives life its spice and value: as *useless* as life itself, yet exalting life as the one end which gives all others their meaning.

And there is more to it. In essence, what is necessary is what we need as social individuals to live in the socio-cultural context of our own civilisation. The necessary is thus the object of needs which all social individuals have in common. Consequently, its definition can be based on collective decisions, its production on collective planning and organisation. A society which guarantees for everyone what is necessary (clearly something which will evolve with the society itself) in exchange for the amount of work required for its social production does not encroach on individuals' spheres of potential autonomy. Instead it minimises the sphere of necessity and the work which goes with it, leaving each individual free to define and produce in his or her own way all that is optional and inessential.

The situation is altogether different when society makes no distinction between the production of necessities and inessentials, by subjecting both to central planning or to the law of the market and private enterprise. In either case, the unity of the economy rules out any separation between labour which produces necessities and labour which produces inessentials. Labour power is expended and paid for at the same rate for both: for a section of the population, only the production of inessentials allows them access to necessities. They cannot reduce this non-necessary production in order to cut their work time. This, in fact, is the situation we live in today.

Furthermore, determining which inessentials should be produced remains a matter for institutional decision-making rather than free individual choice – and thus encroaches on and reduces individuals' spheres of autonomy. We become the objects of institutional socialisation even in our tastes, our pleasures, our luxuries and our free-time activity. Ultimately, the tendency is towards the model outlined earlier, where commodities buy their consumers, fostering a strategy of normalisation, autosurveillance and social control of even the most intimate aspects of our behaviour.

For all these reasons it is clear that a drastic reduction of work time and a guaranteed social income for life will extend the sphere of autonomy only within the framework of a pluralist economy where obligatory work (approximately 20,000 hours in a lifetime) produces only necessities, while all non-necessities depend on autonomous, self-determined, optional activity.

25. Connections and overlaps, innovations and self-management

The necessary encompasses all that social individuals need to live and all that society needs to function: public and collective services and resources, infrastructures and administration, consumer and general goods. Just like the 'utility goods' in Britain immediately after World War Two, which were given priority in the allocation of raw materials, necessary products are, by definition, functional, durable, repairable, economical in terms of labour and natural resources, as immune to the vagaries of fashion as blue jeans, walking shoes and mopeds, farm machinery or the Citroën 2CV, whilst able to incorporate technological advances.[22]

Ever since the birth of industry, socialist thinkers, and especially Ricardo and Marx, have recognised that reduction of time spent producing necessities is the precondition for any possible liberation. For this reduction allows the expansion of a sphere *in which economic logic no longer applies*. Ricardo and Marx were not mere theoretical economists; they were *critics* of political economy, and could foresee its possible supersession and extinction on the far horizon because (capitalist) development would permit the production of increasing wealth with decreasing social labour.

An anonymous Ricardian socialist, in an admirable text of 1821 to which Marx frequently refers in the *Grundrisse*,[23] sees 'the first indication of a real national wealth and prosperity' in the fact that people can work less. It is ridiculous to believe, the writer adds, that when society's productive capacity reaches its height, it will continue to be fully utilised:

where men heretofore laboured twelve hours they would now labour six, and *this* is national wealth, this is national prosperity. After all their idle sophistry, there is, thank God! no means of adding to *the wealth of a nation* but by adding to the facilities of living: so that wealth is liberty – liberty to seek recreation – liberty to enjoy life – liberty to improve the mind: it is disposable time and nothing more. Whenever a society shall have arrived at this point, whether the individuals that compose it shall, for these six hours, bask in the sun, or sleep in the shade, or idle, or play, or invest their labour in things with which it perishes, which last is a necessary consequence if they will labour at all, *ought to be* in the election of every man individually.[24]

Here, and subsequently in Marx's own writings, *economic* activity, that is, work, obeys economic principles only in order to minimise the scope of the economy: henceforth the organisation and management of necessary production aims at reducing as far as possible the time devoted to it. Time is seen as the most precious of resources, and the guiding principle of the sphere of necessity's economy will be to minimise work time so as to maximise disposable time. So the most effective means to achieve high productivity will indeed be sought – but this quest has nothing to do with productivism. The aim is no longer to maximise output and profit, but to free as much time as possible, to increase non-work and non-production.

Certainly no one should be prevented from producing necessities in their disposable time if that is what they want to do. In fact it is all the more likely that institutional production will be partially replaced by autoproduction since a politics of freeing time only makes sense if it provides everyone with workshops – in towns, neighbourhoods and even apartment blocks – which can offer an increasingly wide range of tools and materials for creativity, repair- and assembly-work and autoproduction.[25]

But necessities produced in your free time always have a different status from those which *have* to be produced. Precisely because the latter are guaranteed to all by society, the former are extras which you make for the sheer pleasure of creating them by yourself, indulgences, not things which you couldn't do without. Bread and cakes you bake yourself are not the same as those you buy; handmade clothes and shoes have a different appeal from those made in a factory. When you make things for pleasure you do not count up the time it takes: it is simply another part of life itself.

Between institutional production and autoproduction for pleasure by individuals and neighbours, we must, however, introduce a third level: small-scale free enterprise, either co-operative or communal. After all, the desire to invent, innovate or pioneer is no less legitimate than the desire to write books, make films or compose music. And its satisfaction cannot be left to the limited outlets afforded by institutional production.

For the latter, it already plays a fundamental role – as a stimulus, a complement or a competitor. Most innovations come from small businesses, often started (especially in the United States) by a team of two or three ex-academics or consultant engineers who have quit their jobs in industry, or (as in Italy) by a factory supervisor who has studied at evening classes and then left the giant factory taking along a handful of skilled workers.[26]

Institutional production's only lasting protection against bureaucratic rigidity will be the free exercise of entrepreneurial pioneering, which is not something specific to capitalism. Financial reward is not, or need not be, a fundamental motivation for innovators any more than it is for artists or mountaineers, researchers or inventors. The urge to innovate, to start a business, is just the same as any other creative urge. And, like all other forms of creativity, it sets up its own criteria for success and then tries to gain recognition for them.

Only in the world of capitalism is commercial and financial success the condition and the yardstick for success in general. As a result, the way innovators and innovations are selected and evaluated discourages most people with creative potential from entrepreneurial activity: the ferocity of the 'business world' deters them. Innovative ability, therefore, will be more freely deployed outside the constraints of a capitalist economy. Competition does not need to be a fight to the finish in order to be effective: it could, for example, take the form of a kind of Olympic Games for innovators. The social criterion for success, instead of being financial, could be the ability to 'attract imitators', to gain the interest and attention of colleagues or potential innovators by giving exhibitions and presentations or lecturing at the numerous 'open universities' where everyone can provide, acquire or exchange knowledge.

Furthermore, an enterprise does not have to be capitalist to be independent and effective: it can remain a personal venture while operating under the communal control of, or under contract to, a local authority which provides its capital. Like the workers' co-ops and small craft enterprises in Italy's Emilia-Romagna, it can obtain capital, management expertise and even some technical assistance from services set up by the town or region for the specific benefit of small enterprises whose founders have no wish to be employers or capitalists. Or, finally, it can be a venture of the community itself, like the workshops of socialist kibbutzim.

Entrepreneurial aims, moreover, can be of two sorts: either to provide locally some optional goods or services meeting specific local desires; or to carry out locally some socially necessary productions in different, better ways, with lower labour costs.[27] In the latter case, the enterprise will be recognised as a social utility – a principal supplier or local subcontractor – and the work put in by its personnel will consequently count towards the quota for their guaranteed lifelong income. In the former, it will really be an association of autoproducers, exchanging some or all of its output with the local community.

For an example of how this exchange would work, Nordal Akerman[28] describes a system originating in Quebec which was introduced some years ago in Sweden: a union of local co-ops, bringing together an ever-widening range of products and services, and entitling all its members to the equivalent of the hours they have given to the community in the form of goods or services. The union will provide, for example, a voucher for holiday accommodation, the services of painters or plasterers, consumer goods or materials, in exchange for a given number of hours' work for the co-op or community. These hours can be worked by individuals, groups or families intermittently or occasionally according to respective needs and opportunities. Monetary relations are thus abolished: exchange assumes a non-market form. And the old marxist maxim becomes everyday reality: 'From each according to his abilities, to each according to his needs.'

What needs to be done, or what the community or its individual members deem desirable, thus no longer relies on uncertain public or private financing. And most things which could not be done before, because of the high hourly labour costs involved, became possible once again: the provision, maintenance, embellishment and improvement of public facilities, neighbourhoods and buildings; forest clearance; neighbourhood services; running repairs to items in daily use; local science shops and medical centres to investigate particular health and scientific problems brought up by neighbourhoods or communities; assistance for the sick or the handicapped, etc. Everyone, in this way, will have three levels of activity:

1) Heteronomous, macro-social work, organised across society as a whole, enabling it to function and providing for basic needs;

2) Micro-social activity, self-organised on a local level and based on voluntary participation, except where it replaces macro-social work in providing for basic needs;

3) Autonomous activity which corresponds to the particular desires and projects of individuals, families and small groups.

As an intermediary level connecting socially necessary, hetero-nomous work and autonomous activity entirely determined by individual choice, the second level thus constitutes the social fabric of civil society. It is the level of debates and trade-offs; the level where decisions are reached as to what is necessary and what is desirable; the level of conflicts and plans for the future, of the 'production of society' in Alain Touraine's sense. Second-level activity will be heteronomous or autonomous according to its objects (necessities or options), the tools employed, the size of the group performing it, and the role it plays in the group's life.

Thus, every local community will have to decide for itself whether, and to what extent, it wants to take on necessary production by substituting micro-social activity for some part of macro-social work. A total substitution, as desired by a section of the self-management movement, will never be possible. Nor is it desirable, for it would subject local communities to the constraints of the sphere of necessity in their organisation and their lives; it would restrict the space for mobility, interchange and autonomous choice. A community whose survival depends on tight integration is not a place where individual liberties will flourish.[29] For these liberties can exist only if there can be multiple solutions to the same problem, if these solutions are always open to individual and collective arbitration, and, especially, if individuals are free to choose when and how they participate in community activity. The to-and-fro between heteronomous work, optional, micro-social activity and autonomous, individual activity makes for balanced lives and individual freedom. Complexity and variety, connections and overlaps, keep open spaces for initiative and imagination. They are what make life worth living.

By way of a conclusion: individual, society, state*

In what circumstances can we call an individual 'autonomous'? And how is that autonomy expressed in his or her social relations?

We can call someone autonomous when s/he conceives and carries out a personal project whose goals s/he has invented and whose criteria for success are not socially predetermined. The term comes from the Greek: 'he who makes his own laws'. By its very nature, autonomous behaviour cannot be explained sociologically. Of course it always occurs within a socially determined field, with socially pre-given instruments. But both are reshaped in unforeseen ways to fit the requirements of a personal venture.

This applies especially – but not exclusively – to those we call 'creators', be they artists, mathematicians, inventors, entrepreneurs, philosophers or militant advocates of new ways of life, new educational models, etc. They are always violating the norms and codes of their society. Which is precisely why they are attacked by rigidly integrated societies and totalitarian states: they are seen as 'asocial' and 'immoral', as threats to the established order and so on, and they are persecuted because of it.

Autonomy necessarily involves solitude, in the existential sense; that is, the consciousness – which phenomenologists call the 'cogito' – that I cannot get others to share my personal convictions and, conversely, that I cannot interiorise the determinants of my social being or live them as personal truths. In short, social existence inevitably carries a degree of alienation because we do not and cannot recognise society as something we have freely created through voluntary co-operation with everyone else.

At the beginning of Malraux's *Les Conquerants* there is an

---

* This interview was first published in the journal *Autogestions* No. 8/9, and was conducted by Olivier Corpet, Jocelyne Gaudin, Michael Grupp and Bruno Mattei.

extract from a police file on Garine, a professional revolutionary, which includes his own self-description: 'I am asocial as I am atheist'. I love that phrase. For the believer believes that beyond his own thought there is an absolute, true thought that thinks *him*, and with which he desperately tries to align his own. In just the same way, people who follow the dominant norms and values of their social milieu regard society as an all-engulfing subject which thinks *them* according to its own transcendent truth. There is a certain religiosity in any attitude which holds that individuals must serve society and be the instruments of its integrity. And there is always something anomic about such attitudes: whatever shape it takes, law and order is considered to be something intangible to which we must submit with a passive or competitive conformism. On the other hand, he who feels committed to be the only judge of Good and Evil, is 'asocial as he is atheist' – he wants society to serve individual development by the wealth of materials and spaces it provides for creativity.

But what makes some individuals more autonomous than others?

Above all family background. There is that famous study by Kornhauser in the United States which shows that individuals whose work is repetitive and without scope for initiative are more anomic (that is, lacking autonomy and submissive to hierarchies). But this apparent social determinism has obvious limitations. First of all, there are all those who do repetitive, semi-skilled jobs temporarily in order to get money for personal projects. This is particularly common in the United States where lots of people do unskilled work to pay their way through college. In France, André Schwartz-Bart took a semi-skilled job at Renault so he could write the prize-winning *The Last of the Just*.

Moreover, since Kornhauser published his study we have witnessed the spread of a worldwide revolt by semi-skilled workers, especially by the young ones. And here the social factors don't explain very much: there has been a cultural mutation, that is, a change in the perception of work, of oneself as a worker, of what is acceptable and what isn't. Now this cultural relation of individuals to the social world is formed above all in the family context: by reacting against it rather than conforming to it. The more contradictory the family background, the more it becomes impossible to follow its values, or even to see any values to follow – and so the more the child is forced to be autonomous. To achieve this autonomy, the child will still need cultural support, which in our society only the parents or their substitutes can provide. On the whole, autonomous individuals, particularly 'creators', artists, intellectuals and so on, most often come from families where parental authority is absent or inadequate, and where someone else provides a taste for ideas, books, art, or simply encourages curiosity.

In short, autonomous individuals are those whose socialisation has been defective, incomplete – where the non-socialised part of their lives prevails over the socialised part. To them, society, *any* society, seems something contingent, almost accidental, somewhat absurd, certainly *external*. They are always aware that the norms and laws which run society don't correspond to their personal, moral or aesthetic needs and convictions or to their relationships with others. Whatever the society, alienation is insurmountable.

And we really can't eliminate this alienation?

It can be reduced, its real significance can be limited but, no, it cannot be completely eliminated. On the contrary, I think that claiming that it can be only leads to denying it, and that denial is a characteristic of totalitarianism, including socialist totalitarianism. One way or another, the latter always proclaims: 'We live in the best of all possible societies, all men are equal, all are brothers, so if you are unhappy, if you don't wholeheartedly identify with your social role, it's because you are maladjusted, or insane, a troublemaker or a criminal, maybe even an imperialist lackey and enemy of the people.'

Whatever the political regime, every society is in some respects a giant machine requiring individuals to respond promptly to technical imperatives whose performance is basically tedious and ungratifying. In China, for example, one such imperative is to empty the latrines over the fields as manure. If that's what is necessary, you can take one of two attitudes: you can say, OK, this is lousy drudgery that no one wants to do, so we'll share it out so that no one has to do it for very long; but, as happened in China, you can also start from the principle that common interest in the Triumph of the Great Proletarian Revolution demands that everyone identifies with the collective cause, renouncing his or her own needs the better to serve society. Then the good citizen becomes the heroic worker who happily sacrifices him or herself to the Revolution, and whose greatest personal satisfaction is found in shovelling shit. It's no longer drudgery: it's a moral and civic duty. Good citizens enjoy spreading manure. And as there are certain people, such as intellectuals, who there is every reason to believe don't like this kind of work, well then they must be the first to do it, and must sing its glory into the bargain, giving thanks to the Great Leader who has enabled them to discover the joys of this particular form of self-abnegation.

Till now, all socialist regimes have instituted this religion of work, and tried to deny its alienation by glorifying it. If work were really so uplifting and ennobling, there would be no need to glorify it. But of course the truth is that it hasn't changed at all, and any society based on large units of production, be it socialist or capitalist, retains the aspect of a giant machine in which people are the servants of vast systems of material production, rather than the systems being the servants of everyone's personal development.

But by developing autonomous work isn't it precisely the material reorganisation of society that you're trying to tackle, to eliminate this aspect of a giant machine? Isn't the real goal to break down everything which is too big to be self-managed in order to rediscover autonomous work? The idea of autonomous work clearly includes the notion of a return to a meaningful, lived relationship between the needs of the individual and the group and its production, to mutual exchange. How far, then, can this sphere of autonomy extend? For what economic, social or political reasons would there be an ultimate limit to this growth, whatever the direction of history?

If I stress the fact that every society in part resembles a giant machine which for individuals will always include a degree of social alienation, it is precisely so that, starting from this recognition, we can endeavour to minimise the institutions, the 'tools' in Illich's sense, and the activities which presuppose and maintain this giant machine. But we will never eliminate them completely: for if the sphere of autonomy is to be without any external limit, the world would have to be exclusively composed of small enterprises, self-managed by their members in free co-operation – little islands of perfection. Which would roughly correspond to primitive societies, like those which existed until recently, totally isolated from the world and each other, in Amazonia.

Autonomous production is essentially handicraft production in which the individual or the 'convivial' group controls the means of production, the labour process and the nature and quality of the product itself. But for us it is out of the question to return to the spinning-wheel, the water-mill and the domestic or village economy in order to meet all or even most of our needs. Today's autonomous production uses or will use for the most part sophisticated, high-performance tools which any group or individual can master but which cannot be manufactured at group or local level. Microprocessors, for example, and even bicycles or the components of a solar heating system (not to speak of photoelectric cells) presuppose a division of labour on a national or even continental scale. They require highly sophisticated metallurgy, optical instruments, advanced chemistry, electro-chemistry, bearings manufactured with specialised machinery, etc.

No single group or individual can master all the different technologies that are needed to make a bicycle or a mini-robot. So to provide these tools we need people and production units specialising in the conception and manufacture of parts and components with no use value in themselves: microchips, say, or bicycle chains. Inevitably these people will lose control over what they produce. Their production is part of a much wider system which they cannot affect in their own work. Their work can have a limited degree of autonomy, it can be skilled, pleasant and so on, but it will not be an autonomous activity. Its destiny is first and foremost to serve the *market*, not their colleagues or the local community. By this I mean that such work will be rewarded in terms of its value in Marx's sense: working hours are exchanged, use values are not. In return for the labour I provide, I receive a wage which, if exploitation is abolished, will allow me to buy things representing an equivalent number of labour hours. Commodity relations aren't abolished, nor is wage alienation nor external determination of the nature and specifications of the products I help to produce. Socialism alters nothing. At best it can allow workers to determine their working conditions in the broadest sense.

Thus the sphere of autonomy is in fact always based on the existence of a sphere of socialised, heteronomous production. It is only through the latter's efficiency and productivity that we can obtain the tools and the time for a flourishing autonomy and a rich and varied range of possible activities. If it wasn't for the sphere of social production with its division of labour and relatively large and complex production units we would have to work a great deal more to produce the bare necessities.

But what kind of work would this be? Wouldn't it precisely be more autonomous?

Yes and no. In peasant-artisan society people were more autonomous in as much as they were controllers of their own time, of the rhythm and method of their own work. But this autonomy wasn't experienced as such when people worked from dawn to dusk for their subsistence, often with no reserves of any kind. What is rewarding about today's autonomous activities, using 'convivial' tools and technology, is that they give you a rest from heteronomous work, are characteristically creative and subversive: in a society dominated by large-scale market production you can cut out little islands which provide alternative social and cultural models. But if these were dominant, if we were legally obliged to spend most of our time working with 'soft' technologies at home or in the community, we wouldn't find it at all creative or rewarding.

And it would also be a contradiction in terms – because a principle of centralisation would be being applied to something which should precisely go against that principle.

The state does not need to be centralised to impose legally binding norms: it simply has to pressure people into conformity, as is the case in China especially. If political authority established the principle that good citizens are those who, whether in the family or the small co-op, make their own clothes, grow their own vegetables and build their own solar converter and wind-pump, under threat of moral and material sanctions, then you have a stifling, repressive, ultra-conformist, authoritarian society even if as in China, centralisation remains undeveloped.

For me, the only real autonomous activity is one that is neither an obligation imposed in the name of moral, religious or political principles, nor a necessity for survival. But if it isn't to be either of these, subsistence must be taken care of by an advanced system of social production which provides all we need to live and demands only a small fraction of our time.

There is still something disturbing about this model, for the more we reduce the work needed for essential production, the more vital such work becomes and the more the hyper-productive sector grows in importance. It becomes the centre of attention because it has to play 'foster parent' to everything else. And so the danger is that its productivist values will dominate all other social activity.

No, things really don't happen like that. The desire for high productivity doesn't always imply a productivist ethos. Productivism is when you say production has got to get faster and faster so we can produce more and more, because more equals better. But if you say we must produce the maximum in the minimum time so that we all have the time to do what we want – that's not productivism. Because then the goal isn't to increase production; it's to increase free time. Productivity is simply a means to this end. And it rests on the search for higher-performance tools and equipment, not on glorifying effort. Antiproductivism should not be equated with contempt for technology and rationality.

Moreover, if we look at the evolution of the most advanced countries, North America in particular, we can see that the growth of technological productivity goes hand in hand with a cultural mutation: free time tends to become more important than work, the use value of time (what you can do for yourself) much more important than its exchange value (what you can get by selling your time). This evolution is clearly more marked among people who have had more education, and this is so not because they have higher incomes but because they have, culturally, more autonomy. They want to, and can, fill their own time, which isn't so true of people who have always done repetitive work for 48 hours or more a week.

But it's still a real cultural mutation. Cultural change always starts with the most educated social strata. It will spread all the more rapidly when a politics of time allows everyone to fill their own free time in self-fulfilling or creative ways.

Which is still not the case in the United States. Nothing there suggests that the ideology of work is being put into question. On the contrary, the drastic reduction of work time which has put 10 per cent of the population on the dole is perhaps not creating an aversion to work so much as a renewed attachment to traditional values.

What is happening is that industrial society is doing its best to hide the fact that the amount of socially necessary labour is declining rapidly and that everyone could benefit from this. Instead of proposing more free time for all those who want it, the only choice being offered is between full-time work or full-time unemployment – which is a way of presenting free time as a disaster, as social death. What is more, except in Scandinavia, those who are unemployed, retired or retired early are not allowed to be autoproductive, because whatever they produce for themselves and their friends reduces the outlets for commodity production. Faced with the alternatives 'full-time work' or 'dole' people still prefer work. Which does not mean that they still value work in the traditional way.

On the contrary, as we can see in the United States and Northern Europe, and as the studies quoted by Guy Aznar in *Tous à Mi-Temps*! ('Part-time for All!') showed, there is a strong, but unsatisfied demand for free time: a very significant proportion of the active population attach more importance to their autonomous activities than to their waged work. The cultural mutation is clearly here already but society continues to block its social and political emergence. That is why I'm saying we need a political struggle for society to give people both the right and the material possibility to attach at least as much importance to autonomous activity as to socially predetermined waged work. In any case, technological evolution is abolishing vast amounts of work and confronts society with a choice: a society of unemployment still productivist and grossly unequal, or a society of free time where self-determined, non-market activities predominate over waged work with economic goals.

Alvin Toffler, in *The Third Wave* has shown very clearly how the micro-electronic revolution can herald a civilisation where economic goals, market production and monetary exchange will once again become secondary. But obviously this objective possibility will become reality only if it is backed by a political will. Why shouldn't that happen? We live in an extraordinarily schizophrenic way. Our social relations are dominated by the notion of equal exchange, yet this notion, shared by both capitalism and socialism, is missing from our existential experience. In our personal and emotional relationships there is never any question of equal exchange; it is always a matter of giving more than we receive. Relationships of friendship, love, affection and tenderness are based on our desire to give the other as much as possible, to give everything – it's as if we compete to give more. And that is how it is in primitive societies: competitive generosity. At this level, economic goals and market values don't exist.

All the same, every real exchange has an element of mutual interest. Both partners gain from it.

Once you start thinking about interest, you're lost. If I have an interest in loving you, I don't love you.

Indeed, but it's not easy to go from relationships between two or three people to social relations on a much wider scale. The example of loving relationships or primitive societies is hard to extend to a whole society.

That's exactly what I'm saying. In our societies social relations are cold, codified, legalistic and mechanical – no one has any personal investment in them and that's why there is this gulf between personal existence and social existence. Hence the current quest for warmth in social relations, for ways of breaking free from economic goals and imperatives.

But if spontaneous or autonomous relations between individuals are different from social relations, we have to admit that the latter are necessarily codified or even imposed by external rules.

That is indeed what happens. In the United States during the 1970s there was intense discussion in the communes about the size of a group which was compatible with warm, open relations. The definition reached by the movement in California was that a group ceases to be the subject of its members' reciprocal relationships and initiatives when it is no longer possible to talk to all your fellow members in a conversational tone. When whoever is talking has to give a speech or a lecture then relations of reciprocity and spontaneous exchange have been superseded by a system of relations involving all the problems of hierarchies, domination, rivalry and so on.

At the end of the 1960s and beginning of the 1970s, there were fierce debates in many places between those who believed all power should be vested in mass assemblies and those who believed in the central role of organisations. The former opposed any delegation of responsibility, advocated mass initiatives and rejected all hierarchies. The latter argued that the apparent spontaneity of such assemblies in reality left the field open for certain kinds of charismatic leaders who would take and hold power through all sorts of undemocratic methods, including intimidation, blackmail and terror. Which proved to be the case. In collectives which are larger than 'convivial' groups, members' freedom and equality can be preserved only if the running of the collective is governed by rules and procedures that apply to everyone; that are recognised as Law.

But who is going to make these laws and who is going to enforce them?

In practice, laws are ideally drawn up by specialised sub-groups or 'committees' delegated by the collective as a whole during assemblies. Parties are supposed to function in the same way, but as we know, they rarely do, in particular because of the influence that their participation in government and elections has on their mode of operation. In theory, civil society – the fabric of real, lived social relations – should be the only source of law.

In your book Farewell to the Working Class *you distinguish two spheres: that of autonomy, which you've also just called the sphere of warm or convivial relations; and the sphere of heteronomy which you've just called the sphere of cold, social relations, codified according to the functional imperatives of collectives whose size rules out the possibilities open to associations of individuals. You demand that these functional imperatives be codified into rules of law which the state, according to you, must enforce. At the same time you want to see the sphere of heteronomy and the state reduced to a minimum. How can the state be reduced to a minimum while exercising a decisive social role? Following the perspectives of self-management, shouldn't we analyse the state as the 'superior' social form which bends all other forms into submission?*

Here we have two quite different problems. First of all, the size of the state depends on the size of the sphere of heteronomy, which itself depends on the material structures of the country as a whole. The heavier the technology and the more production is technically and economically concentrated, the more society runs like a giant machine, like one big factory. Its control requires quasi-military organisation – which is provided by the state and its institutions. Self-management of the economic machine in its present form is inconceivable. Self-management of a national railway system is meaningless. The form and functioning of both of them is statist, bureaucratic, military. We can certainly reduce their importance by transferring a greater proportion of energy production and transport to local administrations, for example. But there is a limit: rail networks and electricity grids must *also* be nationwide, not simply local.

So the possibility of reducing the sphere of the state depends on how far we can reduce and decentralise technical and economic units. Clearly the state itself has no interest in encouraging this since it would diminish its power. But civil society and the people do have an interest in it, though not one which goes as far as abolishing the state. There is still an irreducible sphere that must be the state's responsibility, not only materially but juridically.

In France, the further left you are, the more you're against the state. This isn't true everywhere. The French state is something that has always been there and has always crushed civil society more than it has protected it. But in Italy, the United States and, especially, Germany, it is the absence of a state which has blocked the development of civil society by allowing the rule of 'princes' to perpetuate itself outside the rule of law. Thus in German philosophy the state was the precondition for laws which would protect both individuals and civil society from the arbitrary rule of princes. We should therefore see the state as the instrument and guarantor of the law, but not its source. Its source must always be social relations themselves.

So you distinguish the state on one side, civil society on the other, and, somewhere between the two, politics, which you say will control their relationship. But in a concrete sense, what would this political authority be like?

It would be like those institutions that we no longer dare to call parties, since they work so badly nowadays. In principle, parties should be associations of citizens who are aware that the need for maximum individual and local autonomy can be met only by translating it into political terms: how the city should be organised, how civil society should work, and how law should codify all that cannot be left to the absolute control of individuals and local communities. In short, politics is taken on by militants who are willing and able to understand social conflicts in legal and organisational terms.

These militants seem very like professional intellectuals who speak in the name of power and may even monopolise it. How should we view their role in relation to civil society?

They translate and formulate the emergent aspirations of civil society and try to make them coherent, effective, compatible with the functioning of the, or *of a*, social system. In principle, every party is a place for discussion and opposition, where everything is openly debated under the control of all those who want to control, and where people can always recall those who aren't representing, or are inadequately representing, their real aspirations.

But there are no examples of parties which work like that.

That is exactly what I said at the beginning. Parties don't work properly because the state is swallowing up society. Today's parties, whichever they may be, transmit the will of the state to the people, instead of the reverse. The party of the majority is the transmission belt for the head of state and the government, with just enough disagreement for it not to be too blatantly obvious. It doesn't develop or represent anything at all. The only citizens' organisations which still do the work which parties should do are study groups, clubs, little groups of trade union militants and so on. Politics is withering away.

Politics should never be confused with executive power, with administration, in other words, with the state. If it is not a means of expression which transmits the aspirations of civil society to the government and challenges the latter in the name of the former and, conversely, the former in the name of a coherent overall view, then politics loses its autonomy, and goes into decline.

But the perspectives of self-management are fundamentally anti-state and thus incompatible with this preservation of a mediating political authority. Doesn't your conception actually lead to a radical revision of the aims of self-management?

The aims of self-management are aspirations, not a global, coherent and operational conception of the nature and functioning of society. Self-management is not possible in communities of more than a few hundred people. But who is to control relations between the different self-managed communities? And who controls the *system of relations* between all the communities which make up a country? And the relations between these systems of relations?

Either you reply 'no one', and thus abandon these relations to what are called 'market forces', which are actually relations of competing powers. Or you can try to civilise, to regulate these relations by public rules which maximise the sphere of autonomy. And in that case you need a legal system, and a state.

There is no third way. Self-management is an aspiration whose effective sphere can be very wide, but it isn't a solution to everything. As an individual, I really don't want to be constantly bothered by all the problems of society, from international exchange to transport and communications systems, from monetary circulation to the police. I don't believe anyone should be forced to spend all their time worrying about such things.

Which clearly implies that we leave it to a class of professionals.

I have nothing against professionals. They will always be there. There will always be surgeons, for example. The only question is how we stop them forming a class or caste, how we stop them doing nothing but exercise and monopolise their skills, thus turning these into a source of power. Of necessity, there will always be people who, in one field or another, know a lot more than others. It takes at least 10 years to make a good agronomist or a good chemist, and even then they will have understood only a relatively small part of agronomy or chemistry. The same goes for geologists, mechanics, legal experts, managers . . . Each of us can't be anything and everything unless we revert to neolithic technology and not even then.

The solution is to reduce the time taken up by socially determined work: let no one exercise their profession for more than an average of four hours a day. As a result, a lot more people will be able to acquire advanced skills and knowledge and public responsibilities. And, since during the rest of their time, they will be equal members of their local community (rather like the way some kibbutzim operate), without any privileges, doing odd jobs, gardening, teaching and learning, looking after the children and doing the cooking just like everyone else, they won't see themselves, or be seen, as figures of authority. It is not specialisation or professionalism that restricts freedom, communication and mobility, it is the privileged status and powers which, in our hierarchical society, go with certain professions. We can get rid of stratification and hierarchy without getting rid of specialisation and the division of skills.

Supplementary Texts

I. *The Third Wave* according to Alvin Toffler*

We are living through the final death-throes of industrialism. This social order, founded upon the religion of work, power, the commodity, standardisation, is in the process of being overwhelmed and buried by a new one, a civilisation of which we have as yet only an approximate, confusing profile. This is Alvin Toffler's central thesis.[1] He writes of the collapse of 400-year-old certainties and evokes the birth of a culture without norms, without hierarchies, without timetables; where the family no longer consists of mum, dad and the kids but includes all possible sex and age combinations; where we produce for ourselves, as members of a family or a co-operative, many of the things which nowadays we buy with money; where there are no more political parties or parliamentary majorities but only ephemeral, changing alliances, linking a multiplicity of minorities on the basis of specific goals.

Do you want proof that this is really the meaning of the present transformation? Would you like a rigorous demonstration showing that industrial civilisation is doomed – even as it defends itself with the frenzy of despair – and that the crisis, barring an outcome of barbarism and dictatorship, is 'pregnant with a civilisation so revolutionary that it undermines all our habitual predicates'? If so you might as well be warned straight away: you won't find in Toffler the irrefutable proof of his thesis. Not only is he unconcerned to derive his argument from an empirical analysis of the facts but he also recalls with some justice that, even in the exact sciences, contrary to legend, new theories are almost never born from empirical observation. Quite the opposite: the great 'discoveries' most often result from the invention of new theories. It is thanks to the latter that certain facts suddenly come to light and

* Translated by Eamonn McArdle. This article originally appeared in *Le Nouvel Observateur*, 29.9.80.

acquire a capital importance, facts which, until the appearance of the new theory, even when they stared the observer in the face, were excluded from the field of observation and judged to be insignificant.

The same thing applies to the deciphering of the contemporary world, of 'history in the making'. In spite of all his scientific language it wasn't on the basis of empirical observation that Marx, in 1848, could argue that the minority class of factory workers was the standard bearer of the society of the future. Toffler, likewise, cannot claim to deduce from empirical observation the final agony of one world and the laboured birth of a civilisation which bears little resemblance to it. Instead this historian of the future invites us first of all to try the keys which he offers without asking him for proof at each step. It is by the doors that they open, by the thousand disparate observations which they allow to connect and acquire significance that these keys will, he thinks, convince us of the truth of his thesis, which is:

> the decisive conflict today is not that between capitalist and communist regimes, but between on the one side, the left wing and right wing 'reactionaries' who want to preserve the industrialist order at any cost, and, on the other side, the growing millions who recognise that the most urgent problems of the world – food, energy, arms control, population, poverty, resources, ecology, climate, the problems of the aged, the breakdown of urban community, the need for productive, rewarding work – can no longer be resolved within the framework of the industrial order.

For the truth is that nothing works as before any longer: in education, medicine, postal communications, transport systems and social security, everywhere the story is the same. Big business is in crisis, its cadres demoralised or beset by gnawing doubts, while miniscule semi-individual enterprises overtake the corporations in most leading sectors. The managing director of one of the world's chemical giants, Hoechst, resigns and goes to live on an Indonesian island because, he says, 'I feel life escaping from me.' Faith in work and the religion of efficiency, growth and progress collapse even within the ruling classes where, in their own hearts, everyone is convinced that 'things can't go on like this' and yet everyone goes through the motions. Science itself is in serious trouble: one of its main pillars, the concept of causality, is collapsing. In the natural as in the social sciences, the idea takes hold (the Chinese have known it for a long time) that minor 'causes' can engender major effects. The whole uniform, linear, mechanistic conception of the physical and social universe is shaken; even time and duration are no longer seen as the continuous flow of unities of time which are always and everywhere identical.

In short, along with its material base, the theoretical framework and the values on which the industrial order was founded are crumbling. Toffler notes that this disintegration has not spared the family, which increasingly tends to consist of a single mother or father with children, or a homosexual couple with children, while the life-long 'nuclear' family with its sexual division of labour tends to disappear.

As one might expect, society and the state are disintegrating along with the industrial order. Political parties and their personnel no longer excite anything but 'anger, and still more, contempt and disgust'. In the most developed industrial countries (the United States, Canada, Scandinavia) which are typically five years ahead of the others, the 'consensus', i.e., the agreement of the population on the nature and definition of the great political problems, has vanished. The president of the United States is elected nowadays only by about a quarter of those eligible to vote, and a Swedish or Danish prime minister hardly carries more real popular weight. Shifting, unstable majorities that cut across left-right frontiers are built and then dissolved around issues which the big political parties regard as secondary (euthanasia, homosexuality, nuclear energy, divorce, etc.), but no majority is possible on an overall political programme.

All this, Toffler thinks, is because political institutions have lost their grasp of realities and events. The giant systems created by industrialism give rise to perverse, indeed paradoxical, effects (think of transport, the urban crisis, the crisis of monetary, banking and health systems; think of the ravages caused by the chemical industry and high-tech agriculture), and the interaction between these systems is getting out of control. The enormous information flux produced and set in motion by giant industries and institutions exceeds the capacity for synthesis of the best-equipped administrations and renders them incapable of properly informed decision-making. It is simply no longer possible to master this flux. Overwhelmed by what Ingmar Granstedt calls 'the enormity of the context', even the strategic decision-makers act blindly.[2] A single report from Exxon to the Federal Energy Agency, for example, runs to 445,000 pages or the equivalent of 1,000 large books: enough to keep someone busy, reading full-time, for six years.

This explains why Toffler thinks that leadership henceforth consists simply in providing the illusion of leadership: 'The weakness with which Carter is taxed is not that of a man but of a system of institutions.' 'Acquiring office by promising not much more than "efficient management" . . . the figureheads of the industrial era' are equally impotent to master a flux of events occurring in a manner which seems both disordered and spasmodic. This is underlined when one remembers the extent to which even the most powerful states are vulnerable to the repercussions of local accidents (think of Seveso, Three Mile Island, the *Amoco Cadiz*), or of the isolated actions of nations, or even of groups which are relatively weak from a military point of view (Iran, the Gulf emirates, the Black September organisation). The only security, Toffler suggests, is to be had through breaking up the large, centralised, centralising systems into much smaller sub-units capable of self-management and swift adjustment to change.

If this decentralisation and diversification of society – where a plurality of partial orders co-exists, adjusting to each other by means of successive trade-offs without ever becoming unified – is not thought out, desired and consciously prepared for, the consequence will be inescapable: either society will fragment into anarchy through violent confrontations, or a totalitarian dictatorship, in attempting to re-establish a unified order through the use of terror and constraint, will reproduce the system of 'waste, irresponsibility, inertia, corruption; in short, totalitarian inefficiency', exemplified in the Stalinist and National Socialist state models.

Now the technical-cultural changes currently taking place, Toffler thinks, point clearly in the direction of decentralisation, destandardisation and a diversification of society. No doubt technological change is of itself ambiguous: it can facilitate hyper-centralisation, total police surveillance, media control of thought and behaviour, as well as their opposites. But the paradox is that many of the techniques (telecommunications and computer networks, microcomputers, robotics) which the industrialist order is currently developing in order to perpetuate its domination, can easily be turned against this order and used to hasten its decomposition. The third wave, Toffler thinks, is precisely the subversion and creative redeployment of these technologies in the service of a cultural revolution which has preceded their appearance, and which learns to nourish itself from them.

A good example of it is what Toffler calls the 'demassification of the media'. The media (advertising, press, radio, television) have been, along with school and the 'spectacle' of the street, the main agents of 'massification': that is, the standardisation and homogenisation of tastes, values, culture and behaviour. The mass media, in supplying industry with the consumers needed for its products, faithfully observed its own rule of influencing the public *as a whole* and avoided issues which ran the risk of dividing, shocking or antagonising sections of it. In this way it created and propagated the image of a 'mass individual' or 'average individual' whose opinion was allegedly that of 'everyone'. This mass individual was in reality *no one*, his or her tastes and opinions corresponded to a statistical average different from the vast majority of real individuals. The mass media persuaded the latter that they were guilty deviants.[3] Press and advertising exercised a powerful pressure to conform.

All that is changing at a dizzying speed, says Toffler. The mass-circulation press, like the big radio stations and TV channels, is affected by the disappearance of the consensus which formerly obtained over a range of values, aspirations and major questions: the nation, power, progress, respect for 'experts', economic growth, etc. This disappearance of consensus provokes the decline of the mass media everywhere. All the big dailies and magazines which addressed this mass public have lost a part of their readership since 1965, while the drop in influence of the big radio stations began a short time later, though television's falling audience dates only from 1977. People are not, however, turning away from the media in general, notes Toffler: they are abandoning the popular national dailies in order to read small, local newspapers; they are abandoning the big magazines for more eclectic weeklies or periodicals. These publications do not assume a fictitious consensus on the major questions of the moment; instead they offer a vivid, subjective journalism or address only the enthusiasts in a special area – folk-rock, skateboarding, wind surfing, organic gardening, solar heating, etc.

This development is facilitated by the transformation of printing technology: microprocessors have made it possible to build inexpensive machines for typesetting, printing and duplicating. Instead of requiring special buildings and large capital outlay, these machines can be installed in ordinary offices and used by non-professionals. Any group, sect or association can produce its own magazine. The monopoly of the press barons is broken.

The story is similar for radio stations There are currently 6,500 in the United States (compared to 2,300 in 1950), or one for 38,000 inhabitants. There are one or more local stations for every religious and ethnic minority, for every age group and social stratum, for every musical taste (hard rock, soft rock, punk rock, country rock, soul music, classical music, etc.), for every cultural level of an atomised public – to say nothing of the 25–30 million Citizen's Band sets thanks to which people in the United States can maintain a dialogue (or polylogue) on the air within a radius of eight to 25 kilometres.

The same evolution can be seen in relation to television, audiences for which will have dropped by 50 per cent in 10 years' time, if we are to believe the former president of one large American channel. Thanks to cable TV and home computers the television viewer will no longer have to swallow passively the 'ready-made' programmes offered as the television staple diet. Linked directly by cable to information banks, newspapers, libraries or cine-libraries, the viewer will be able to create his/her own programme instead of simply remaining passive. Cable TV will also facilitate communication, debate, the exchange of information between people thousands of kilometres apart; it will make it possible to take part in meetings and conferences without leaving one's home. Already, 15–20 million American homes are fitted with cable TV.

The new technologies therefore accelerate this atomisation of the public which the break-up of consensus began. In the absence of a consensus and of an authority capable of imposing universal norms, conformism becomes impossible. You can still model your behaviour on that of 'others', but those others are no longer 'everyone': they are sub-groups, ephemeral mini-communities, associations for specific goals which offer you no guarantee of conformity to universal norms.

Surrounded by a culture shattered into disparate fragments and bombarded by a jumble of news, theories, miscellaneous data defying classification or synthesis, the individuals of the third wave, Toffler says, can only survive if 'they learn to make their own categories, their own frameworks, to form their own strings out of the mass of data shot at them by the new media. Instead of merely receiving our mental model of reality we are now compelled to invent and reinvent it continually.' Instead of producing robot-like people, programmed and controllable, the micro-electronic revolution begins by disintegrating all norms and all possible normality.

This disintegration isn't all negative. According to Toffler it corresponds to a 'demassification' which at the same time permits and encourages a new existential autonomy among individuals. The latter can no longer find their emotional, moral and material security guaranteed by their social integration, nor through the benevolent care of authority, organisations or political institutions. None of that is credible any longer. For a growing number of people therefore, their well-being can no longer be secured by external solutions: it is for citizens themselves to tackle their problems and to fashion their lives, their needs, to determine what they will consume and what they will produce, according to criteria which they alone decide.

This new taste for autonomy is also reinforced by present economic and technological change. The length of the working day, for a start, is being rapidly reduced even if the benefits of it are being enjoyed very unequally. Today work time (the time sold for a wage or a salary – including the time spent travelling to and from work) represents one third of the waking day on average over the year. It is likely to represent only one fifth by the end of the century. The desire for an increase in disposable time quickens simultaneously: 88 per cent of German employees would prefer an increase in free time to an increase in salary.

A sizeable number of American, Scandinavian and German companies try to acknowledge this preference by allowing job-sharing and 'à la carte' schedules, or flexi-time. Two people share one job; or, for variety, three or four people share two or three jobs. These people (couples, friends from shared houses, neighbours from the same block, etc.) arrange it among themselves to work during the hours (or days, or weeks) which suit them best. In one of the big German department stores each of the employees decides on the number of hours s/he wants to work in the course of the year, on the periods and times of attendance. Each week anyone may modify their schedule after consulting with colleagues and supervisors. This 'self-management of time' has only advantages for the employer since it reduces absenteeism, fatigue, friction and increases flexibility, efficiency and profits. (You might well conclude from this that instead of fighting flexi-time or job-sharing, the unions, on the contrary, ought to be carefully negotiating the distribution of profits accruing from them.)

The abolition of timetable constraints ('desynchronisation' as Toffler would say) currently enjoyed by one in four German employees is only one of the aspects of 'demassification'. It proceeds in step with the decentralisation, destandardisation and despecialisation of production. The system of mass production of identical goods is almost obsolete. In nearly all industries (chemicals, shipbuilding, mechanical engineering, clothing manufacture, etc.) the applications of microprocessors allow giant plant to be replaced by small production units. Here, machines controlled by reprogrammable computers produce a very large variety of models in small quantities. In the clothing industry the laser-cutting device even permits the manufacture of made-to-measure clothes for the same price paid today for an off-the-peg item.

So local production for local tastes and needs becomes possible again. Better still, thanks to teletext and computers, the majority of white collar jobs and an extensive range of industrial jobs can be transferred to the employee's home and performed without any timetable constraint. Diversified and enriched these jobs can become group activities: for a family or extended family, for a group of neighbours, etc. Already, Toffler tells us, 20 per cent of jobs in the electronics industry, for example, could be transferred to the employees' homes.

The advantage of this sort of transfer would be uncertain if each task remained as narrowly predetermined as in the vast majority of jobs today. According to Toffler nothing of the kind is in store. Information technology gives birth to a range of intelligent, polyvalent machines which abolish the frontier between intellectual and manual work. The reign of 'specialists' is destined to be replaced by that of the rounded amateur overlapping several disciplines and allergic to hierarchical submission. In addition – and here doubtless is the most important change – everyone is going to be able to use the know-how acquired through their work for their own ends.

Nowadays this know-how (that of computer programmers, accountants, skilled workers or even technicians) is almost always quite useless to the employee outside of work. However, teletext and the new tools programmable by microprocessor enable everyone to produce for themselves a large part of what they consume. This is going to enhance greatly the value of free time. It will no longer be only a significant minority, but a majority of people who will discover that you can do a lot more for yourself with 10 or 20 extra hours of free time than with the money you earn in the equivalent time of paid work.

Toffler calls 'prosumers' those people who want to *produce* for themselves at least a part of what they *consume*, and thereby reassert themselves as the sovereign judges of their needs and of the manner of satisfying them. The thousand ways in which this tendency to 'prosumption' shows itself are clearly, for Toffler, the main motor of the revolution that he sketches for us. He notes firstly, in the vast service sector, the rapid decline of the monopoly held by professionals, be they doctors, plumbers, psychotherapists or mechanics. In the field of medical care the women's movement has shown the way. Self-diagnosis, people taking charge of their own health or illnesses, is spreading in a spectacular fashion. The most widely read health periodical in the United States is called *Prevention*. In the States and the UK, self-help groups of sufferers sharing and mutually benefiting from their experience of illness (and of medicine) can be found for diabetes, the major cancers, silicosis, nervous depression, mental illnesses, haemophilia, etc. In addition to these associations of *cross-counselling* there are groups whose members have an unclassifiable problem which is not the exclusive business of any 'specialist': parents of homosexual children, the bereaved, single mothers or fathers, stammerers, would-be suicides, etc.

This development of self-help extends to plumbing, electronics, car repairs, construction work, etc. For years now the highest TV ratings have been achieved by do-it-yourself programmes dealing with thermal insulation, plastering, painting, wiring. A large manufacturer of electrical household equipment has started a free telephone-advice service enabling customers (after the expiry of the guarantee period, obviously) to repair their machines themselves.

Telecomputing can only accelerate this deprofessionalisation and decommercialisation of maintenance work but its effects will also be felt on home assembly or autoproduction of complex goods sold in kit form: furniture, bicycles, cars, radio and video sets, etc.

Already in the construction industry in the United States more than half of the construction materials are bought and used by individuals. More than 70 per cent of power tools are bought by individuals as opposed to 30 per cent 10 years ago.

For Toffler these tendencies provide a foretaste of an economy in which, according to the formula used by Marx (whom Toffler, a former marxist, is careful not to quote), the measure of wealth will be neither money nor work time, but disposable time made productive and creative. 'The old opposition between work and leisure collapses,' Toffler writes ... 'Given home computers, given seeds genetically designed for urban or even apartment agriculture, given cheap home tools for working plastic, given new materials, adhesives and membranes, and given free technical advice available over the telephone (or perhaps flickering on the TV or computer screen),' production for personal use will tend at least partially to supplant production for the market, to undermine the latter, and to 'dynamite our economic system at the same time as our scale of values'. Income (including GNP) will no longer be able to be a measure of the standard of living – if indeed it still can. Already 'millions of people are discovering that it can be economically and psychologically more advantageous to "prosume" than to earn more money'. Co-operatives and groups of co-operatives will give an unprecendented boost to non-monetary exchanges, i.e., to the barter of products or of work-hours.[4]

This transformation will evidently not take place without sharp conflicts, because the withering away of the market and commodity relations radically calls in question all the powers and institutions of contemporary society. 'The stake goes deeper than the alternative "capitalism or socialism",' Toffler writes. And with good cause: this phenomenon, beyond socialism, which appears on the horizon of the withering away of wage labour and of commodity exchange, is precisely what Marx called communism.

In relation to the Third World, Toffler, very much to the point, asks whether the persistent importance of autoproduction, together with the feeble penetration of the money economy and commodity production, would not enable many countries to make the transition directly from pre-industrial to post-industrial civilisation, avoiding the laborious and costly detour of industrialism. Instead of being forced to give way to the megalopolis and its high-pollution, virtually obsolete heavy industries, village communities could, thanks to microprocessors, give to autoproduction an undreamt-of efficiency. The problem of unemployment, wholly insoluble in today's system, would no longer be posed in the same terms, since the notion of unemployment has a meaning (as Gunnar Myrdal has pointed out) only in economies where all autoproduction has been abolished in favour of wage labour and commodity production.

To have shown, as Toffler has done, the potential for individual and collective liberation implicit in the changes presently under way is worth the most intransigent critique of the established system and its vested interests. In response to the mounting crises and the 'totalitarian offensive' that the forces of industrialism will try to launch, Toffler concludes:

> Nowhere . . . is obsolescence more advanced or more dangerous than in our political life. And in no field today do we find less imagination, less experiment, less willingness to contemplate fundamental change . . . The creation of new political structures . . .

will not be the result of the political struggles which continue to occupy the forefront of the institutional stage, nor of a climactic upheaval,

> . . . but . . . a consequence of a thousand innovations and collisions at many levels in many places over a period of decades . . . The responsibility for change . . . lies with us . . . And we can place strategic pressure on existing political systems to accelerate the necessary changes . . . Like the generation of the revolutionary dead, we have a destiny to create.

II Their famine, our food

Are you prepared to eat less, but eat better, if that can reduce world hunger? That is the question being put to us today, for the first time. Up till now we have always been assured that there is no connection between our own over-consumption of meat, fat and sugar, and the under-nourishment of hundreds of millions of people in the Third World. Now, using the opportunity of World Food Day, two organisations, Frères des Hommes and Terre des Hommes,[1] are setting out to undermine our clear consciences.

With support from dozens of experts and hundreds of eye-witness reports, backed up by surveys, charts and statistics, these two organisations show how our over-nourishment causes or aggravates hunger in the rest of the world. Every day, in effect, we are snatching bread from the mouths of the poorest of the poor.

Of course we are not individually or directly to blame (although, as we shall see, we can individually contribute to changing things). The diversion of the world's nutritional resources is organised by major industries, by international brokers, by oil companies and banks who have never asked for our opinion or waited for our consent. But the fact remains that we profit from this diversion; it is reflected in our eating habits. We consume far more than our share of the world's nutritional resources.

Just look at the figures. According to nutritionists, we require a daily intake of 2,400 calories (plus vitamins, proteins and mineral salts) to lead a normal active life. For 13 per cent of Latin Americans, 25 per cent of Africans and 28 per cent of Asians, the daily intake is fewer than 2,200 calories. For 59 per cent of Bengalis, it is fewer than 1,800. For Europeans, it is 3,000.

'World cereal production', writes the World Bank in one of its recent reports, 'is sufficient to provide every man, woman and child with an intake of more than 3,000 calories per day, which is considerably more than is necessary. In order to eliminate malnutrition, we would only need to re-direct 2 per cent of world cereal production to those who need it.' So it is not true that world food resources are in short supply. The truth is that we are grabbing more than our share. With only one quarter of the world's population, the rich countries consume half of world cereal production and a third of the total sea-fish catch. We consume three times as much cereal per head of population than people in poor countries. How do we manage to get through so much grain? Quite simple – half our grain consumption is used for animal fodder. Cattle in the rich countries consume a third of world grain production – as much as 2,000 million people in the Third World. In France, 60 per cent of the cereal crop is given to animals.

But of course we are not stealing these cereals directly from the poor nations . . . or so it might seem at first glance. For the industrialised countries themselves are among the biggest producers and exporters of grain. North America, Argentina, Australia and France provide the bulk of world exports. But anyone who tells us that this grain surplus is the result of our more effective techniques is lying. In reality, the surplus hides a huge shortage of other food supplies. The industrialised world has a grain surplus because it makes Third World labourers produce a vast quantity of food for its own exclusive use. Overall, the rich countries monopolise 25 per cent of the poor countries' land in order to meet their own nutritional requirements.

What is grown on this land? Pineapples, bananas, avocados and strawberries from Africa or Central America are only the latest developments. The bulk of the land we have grabbed is given over to huge plantations of coffee and cocoa; of soya, groundnuts and other oil-yielding crops; of sugar cane and, more recently, cassava.

In Ghana, for example, cocoa takes up no less than 56 per cent of all cultivated land. Groundnuts, in Senegal, take up 52 per cent. Caribbean countries export sugar and fruit in quantities which represent 2,550 calories per inhabitant per day, while their children suffer from malnutrition. The eight sub-Saharan countries, at the height of the catastrophic drought of 1971–73, continued to export two to five times as much protein as they imported in cereal form. In Brazil well over 12 million acres, or a fifth of all cultivated land, is used to grow soya for Western Europe.

Everywhere these cash crops are cultivated, food crops and the population's nutritional standards suffer. Because we take its land for groundnuts, Senegal must import half its rice and all its wheat. Throughout East Africa, food crops of millet, sweet potatoes, etc., are sacrificed to cash crops for which the industrialised world pays, partly at least, in cereals, of which African imports have trebled in 10 years.

The spread of soya plantations in Brazil has forced a reduction in the cultivation of black beans – the main protein source for the poor – to such an extent that the Brazilians' own protein *supplies* have dropped by 6 per cent while *production* of protein has risen by 68 per cent. The situation is the same in Thailand: this country, which not long ago had a substantial rice surplus, today can provide only 1,900 calories per person per day. But it exports six to eight million tons of cassava per year to Europe. The German-Dutch company organising this export hopes to raise the figure to 20 million tons by 1985.

Now cassava which, just like soya, Europe feeds to cattle, can be and has been till now, food for humans. Why is it sold to us as fodder? Why do countries like Brazil, Zaire, Nigeria, Sudan and India, where a large proportion of the population is under-nourished, choose to sell their agricultural produce to rich countries instead of using it to feed themselves? It is certainly not because the peasants benefit from it: their food crops would give them two or three times as much nutrition as the price they get for their cash crops allows them to buy. No, the answer really lies in this blunt statement from Frères des Hommes: 'a Normandy pig or cow, or a Parisian cat or dog, has a greater purchasing power than landless peasants in the Third World.'

This is what we have to understand – growing soya for our cows is more profitable for the big landowners in Brazil than growing black beans for the Brazilian masses. Because our cows' purchasing power has risen above that of the Brazilian poor, soya itself has got so expensive in Brazil that a third of the population can no longer afford to buy either its beans or its oil. This clearly shows that it is not enough to ensure the Third World gets 'a fair price' for its agricultural exports. The relatively high prices that we would guarantee might merely aggravate hunger in the Third World, by inciting the big landowners to evict their share-croppers, buy agricultural machines and produce for export only. Guaranteed higher prices have positive effects only if they can be effectively used to raise the purchasing power of the poor masses.

Can industrialised countries intervene in this way? Indeed they can, and in so doing they would also be acting in the interests of their own people, as we shall see. But to do so they must first put a stop to the organised wastage which underpins our own system of food production and consumption. Europe currently imports 35 million tons per year of oilseed-cake, groundnuts, cotton, soya and other protein-rich crops for animal fodder, all of which (including the new varieties of cottonseed) are equally suitable for human consumption. According to statisticians' calculations, at least 40 million tons of cereal could be harvested, mainly in the Third World, on the land of the protein-rich crops that Europe imports.

Do these imports meet the needs of Europe's own population? Absolutely not, reply the nutritionists. The French are far from being better nourished because they now eat 111 kilos of meat per capita per year, as against 95 kilos in 1970, 80 kilos in 1965, 50 kilos in 1955, 38 kilos in 1900. Quite the opposite. Meat proteins are not the most nutritious: many vegetable proteins have just as much nutritional value.

To appreciate this, we should remember that out of the 20 constituent amino acids of the human body, there are eight which cannot be synthesised by the body itself. These we must obtain from our food, in fixed proportions. If our diet is deficient in a single one of these eight amino acids, then we will suffer nutritional deficiency, however much food we eat – because it will not be assimilated.

To obtain suitable proportions of the eight amino acids, we have become accustomed to eating animal proteins. Yet meat is not the most easily assimilated animal product: only 70 to 75 per cent can be assimilated compared to 85 per cent of dairy produce, 92 per cent of eggs.

Animal products may be the most convenient source of amino acids, but they are not indispensable. We can obtain a fully balanced diet by combining different vegetable products in our meals – chiefly by mixing cereals (which contain a lot of slowly assimilated carbohydrates and 12 per cent protein) with pulses (which contain 25 to 50 per cent protein). Non-European civilisations are well aware of this: they mix couscous or millet with chick

Imports of animal fodder represent:

	Millions of tons of cereal-equivalent	Overseas agricultural land monopolised as a percentage of total agriculture land of importing country
France	5.13	4%
Germany	12	22%
Belgium & Luxembourg	4	59%
Netherlands	11.7	110%

To produce one kilo of	The following quantity of cereal-equivalent (in kilos) is required
Eggs	4.2
Poultry	4.8
Pork	4.8
Mutton	8
Veal	8
Beef	11 to 20

peas or soya, rice or maize with black beans or peanuts, adding vitamin-rich vegetables and spices.[2]

Because it takes between four and 20 kilos of cereals and pulses to obtain one kilo of animal proteins (see chart), meat, till the middle of this century, was considered a luxury, and one which people could easily do without. Factory farming has changed all that. Thanks to the protein-rich crops and to cassava, fish meal and so on, bought cheaply in the Third World, agribusiness multinationals have been able to introduce 'indoor' stock farming. They supply prepared animal feed, precise instructions, shed designs, chicks, piglets, calves and lambs to the 'farmers', from whom they re-purchase the animals when they have reached a standard weight and condition.

The 'farmer', as Bernard Lambert has shown,[3] has become a home-worker, obeying to the letter the instructions of the supplier – who is also his sole customer. From now on, the farm is a factory, processing tens of thousands of chickens which will be slaughtered after 25 days; or hundreds of calves, penned in when they are eight days old, slaughtered 92 days later. Jammed together in air-conditioned pens, unable to move, these animals will never see daylight, never touch the ground. All their instincts are thwarted; only tranquillisers and antibiotics keep them alive, fatted and anaemic.

In the last 25 years, factory farming has reduced the real price of pork, poultry and eggs by 25 to 50 per cent. Only beef prices have risen (by 45 per cent allowing for inflation) since beef stock has to be fattened for three years, eliminating the slaughter of animals at a very early age. Factory-farmed meat has become a basic food, replacing cereals and pulses in our diet.

For the peasantry, this evolution has brought servitude. The farmer has largely become a processor, a prisoner of the factory produce supplied by agribusiness monopolies. Out of every 100 francs farmers earn, they pay 77 to the supplier. Such narrow margins force farmers to produce on a larger and larger scale, but only a very few big farmers can survive. Thus, two thirds of French chickens are now reared in 2,300 factory farms, with over 10,000 chickens each. The number of cattle-sheds holding more than 20 cows has risen by half in six years, but the number of dairy farms has dropped by 25 per cent in the same period. Factory farming may well have saved Breton agriculture, but only by getting rid of farmers. Of the 120,000 farms that remain, half will go when their present owners retire. The same applies to half the 850,000 surviving mixed farms in France.

French peasants, just like those in the Third World, are thus becoming subcontractors for agribusiness monopolies; they no longer have any real control over their farming techniques, their crops or their livestock, while their standard of living continues to deteriorate.

But surely the consumers, at least, are benefiting? Yes, insofar as they have cheap, plentiful food. No, because the standard of their nutrition is falling, their food is unhealthy. Daily per capita consumption is currently 300 grams of meat, 100 grams of sugar and 200 grams of cereal. We eat 330 per cent of the average amount of sugar needed for a healthy diet, 200–300 per cent of the fat, 160–200 per cent of the protein; our calorie intake is 50 per cent too high. On the other hand, our diet is seriously lacking in calcium and fibre, and often in vitamins. Dental caries, cardio-vascular disease, kidney- and gall-stones, varicose veins, haemorrhoids, stomach cancer, etc., are the results,[4] and lead to massive consumption of drugs and medication.

At the other end of the chain the damage is even more costly, for it is more difficult to repair. Factory farming produces huge concentrations of liquid and solid dung which, instead of being spread on the land after ripening into manure, will pollute ditches, streams and the watertable itself. The soil deteriorates for want of manure, and requires ever-increasing applications of chemical fertiliser, whose soluble nitrogen, in turn, pollutes water supplies, to the point where water becomes unfit for human consumption.

Over and above these direct effects, we have to take into account 'side-effects' like the following. Pastures are abandoned, because peasants in mountainous regions cannot compete with factory farms. At the same time, lacking commercial outlets, cultivation of soil-enriching graminaceous and leguminous forage plants (like clover and lucerne) gives way to extensive cultivation of cereals which benefit from guaranteed prices. The result? There is a grain surplus which, unsaleable at its real price, will be sold off at a loss: we subsidise its export, adulteration and use as animal fodder. These subsidies cost European consumers around £250 million.

Milk subsidies are three times as costly. Here, the absurdity of our system reaches its limit:

First stage: thanks to the protein-rich crops imported from the Third World, we save a lot of milk in calf-rearing, while increasing the output of dairy farms. There is a tenfold increase in milk supplies.

Second stage: milk production exceeds Europe's own needs by 10 per cent. The annual surplus would fill a lake one kilometre long by two kilometres wide and five metres deep. The surplus is made into butter or milk powder so it can be stored. No less than 56 per cent of all milk produced in Brittany, for example, is stored in this way.

Third stage: EEC stocks rise to 230 million kilos of milk powder and 350 million kilos of butter – all totally unsaleable. So we sell it off at a loss, through heavy subsidies, to Eastern Europe and, especially, to agribusiness, which uses the milk powder for animal fodder.

Agribusiness has thus plundered the lands of poor countries, subjugated peasants in the West, destroyed nutritional autonomy here and abroad, and left us with the following net result – our battery calves drink rehydrated, reheated milk powder instead of milk from their mothers' udders. The cost of this operation is one litre of petrol (energy) per litre of milk plus £750 million in various subsidies. Total cost of food aid to the Third World: £140 million.

And so the circle is complete. Our bad diet is a result of the plundering of the Third World. Hunger in the Third World is perpetuated by our bad diet. Hence the slogan of Frères des Hommes-Terre des Hommes: 'Eat better here. Conquer hunger overseas.' Here and abroad, free the people, starting with the peasantry, from the stranglehold of the agribusiness multi-nationals. In the West, as in the Third World, re-establish nutritional self-reliance – the capacity of nations to feed themselves.

But where do we start? Three simultaneous actions are needed.

First, we must reduce our imports of protein-rich crops and start rearing animals with the produce of our own land. How? By, for example, transferring to 'natural' rearing (particularly of calves by their mothers) the subsidies which now finance the production, processing and, finally, destruction of milk surpluses, purely for the benefit of industry. Our independence, our balance of trade, our health will all gain from this. Meat will be better – and a little dearer.[5]

Second, we should learn from infancy (or re-learn) to eat less meat, less fat, less sugar. The resulting economies can directly aid the fight against hunger. In Norway, where it is illegal to use wheat for animal fodder, 20,000 citizens have joined the 'Future in Our Hands' movement. They are experimenting with ways of living more frugally and investing all or part of the money thus saved in improvement schemes in the Third World. It is this kind of movement that the campaign by Frères des Hommes-Terre des Hommes is trying to launch in France.[6]

Third, we must gradually stop buying agricultural produce from the Third World and develop food crops there instead of cash crops. We can do this by applying the following form of aid: progressively replace our purchases of protein-rich crops, cassava, etc. by purchases at guaranteed prices of rice, pulses, millet, etc. But France (like other countries) would not take delivery of this produce. Instead, it would send it to agreed depots in the producing country itself – and negotiate with the government concerned a method of collection and distribution that would ensure the local peasantry benefits from the guaranteed price while the poor benefit from the availability of produce.

Unlike gifts of cash or grain which ruin local peasants and profit only speculators, this kind of aid will be genuinely effective. Hunger will be conquered only if we help the world's poor to help themselves.

III. Automation and the politics of time*

The micro-electronic revolution differs from earlier technological revolutions in one essential point: it does not only eliminate the most highly skilled intellectual and manual jobs; it also eliminates the repetitive tasks of unskilled workers in the industrial and tertiary sectors. To stress only the deskilling brought about by this revolution is to mask the specificity and significance of the present transformation. For, though it can indeed be used in some situations to increase domination and control of workers,[1] this transformation is not merely a new, ultra-sophisticated form of assembly-line techniques (Taylorism).

Unlike Taylorism, its principal aim is not to destroy the real power of skilled workers. They have not *had* any real power for the last 50 years: in most cases, skilled workers are just a small island in a sea of unskilled workers. At least four-fifths of wage earners do not have anything like the skills which would give them a real trade, with complete control over what they produce and the whole range of tools they use. The primary goal of automation and computerisation is, instead, to eliminate unskilled jobs (by robotising them) and, additionally, to standardise and homogenise what were previously the most highly skilled jobs. Economies of time (of labour, of personnel) are the main objective, not the reinforcement of control and command.

If hierarchy is downgraded by this transformation, if the functions of supervision and control are suppressed, it is not in order to break the power of those whom Marx called the 'officers and non-coms of production'. Rather it is because the automated systems automate these functions by integrating them into the machine itself. There is indeed a levelling of skills. But this levelling is applied simultaneously at the top and the bottom: the

---

* This text first appeared in *CFDT Aujourd'hui* no. 54, March–April 1982

jobs of supervisors and foremen and the few surviving professionals are eliminated at the same time as those of the mass of unskilled workers are de-specialised, simplified and transformed into maintenance and repair jobs.[2]

Overall, beyond the undermining of traditional skills, it is work itself which tends to be abolished. According to the paper presented by C. Rosen of the Stanford Research Institute to the March 1979 congress of the United Auto Workers, 80 per cent of manual jobs in the United States will be automated before the end of the century (that is, 20 million of the 25 million manual jobs which now exist in the United States). Office jobs will undergo an equally drastic reduction.

This process of the abolition of work cannot be reversed or restrained in the name of the employee's right to exercise a skilled trade. It is precisely because skilled trades have already been eliminated from large-scale socialised production of goods and services that their automation is now possible. The vast majority of jobs are no longer a source of pride or fulfilment for their holders. Under certain conditions, automation can enrich their lives by freeing their time, allowing them to diversify their activities and their centres of interest. In place of a lifetime's subjection to the constraints and fatigue of impoverishing work, automation can create the possibility of a form of work which, by taking up less time, can become just one dimension of a fulfilling life, and not necessarily the main one.[3]

It is not a matter of resigning ourselves to work which remains alienated, impoverishing and boring. Instead, we must:

1. recognise that for most people, work is just that;
2. change it so that that is no longer the case;
3. understand that this change, which for 20 years has been the main objective of the most advanced sections of the labour movement, cannot be achieved in the short term and thus cannot now, in itself, be a goal around which people can be mobilised;
4. recognise that, on the other hand, a reduction in the time and importance we give to alienated work is within our reach; that such a goal is liberatory and can attract mass support; that collective analysis and action towards this end can fundamentally redefine the conditions, content and nature of work.

The politics of time

A drastic reduction in work time, however, is no more intrinsically liberatory than the automation which makes it possible. It will only bring liberation within a social environment which does not yet exist (at least not generally) and if it initiates a politics of time open to continual elaboration and renegotiation.

In our present social environment, only work – however unsatisfactory it may otherwise be – gives men and women the opportunity for collective action, communication and exchange. The sphere of non-work is a place of solitude and isolation, of enforced idleness for all those who live in the outskirts and suburbs of the major cities.

Freed time be nothing but empty time unless there is:

1. A politics of collective facilities, which can provide cities, towns and even apartment blocks with places for communication, interchange and autonomous activity. A possible example would be the community centres which exist in some places in Britain, which bring together under one roof a swimming-pool, library, reading-, music- and play-rooms, cafeteria, and workshops for repairs and do-it-yourself. In some large apartment blocks in Scandinavia, there are communal areas such as kitchen-restaurants, laundries, gyms, meeting-rooms, play-rooms (for children), do-it-yourself workshops. In Sweden, co-ops and/or unions provide workshops and instructors (for carpentry, mechanics, electronics) for their members after work. 'As trade unionists, we must also struggle to ensure that workers have outside work an urban environment which will allow them to develop their free-time activities,' said Michel Rolant, and he proposed that 'union branches in each town or district draw up a plan for collective facilities which would be financed from the 3 to 4 per cent of the total wage bill which each company is presently bound to contribute for "social works", accommodation, adult education, etc.'[4]

2. A politics of voluntary co-operation and association allowing the development of all kinds of local, non-market, collective services, which are more effective, more appropriate and more adaptable, as well as being less expensive, when they are not state-run institutions: child-care co-ops, shared transport, help for

the elderly. At least a part of the money thus saved by the state would be given to these informal co-ops.[5]

Beyond collective and shared self-help, some groups in Britain and the United States have set up informal autoproduction co-ops, 'swop shops' and building co-ops. The latter are based on the exchange of work between people who have come together to learn particular building skills and to help each other build their respective houses.[6] The Swedish sociologist Nordal Akerman[7] advocates the co-operativisation, based on voluntary labour, of local renovation and improvements, as well as local production co-ops for basic goods which would be twinned with farming co-ops; exchange of goods and services, valued according to their required work hours, at least partly replacing monetary exchange.

A politics of time is the key both to work-sharing (that is the sharing out of waged work among all those who want to work) and to a freer life. The same reduction of work time will create jobs or not create them, be cheap or costly, capable of 'changing life' or not, depending on whether, for example, it takes the form of a 35-hour, five-day week and a single shift, plus longer annual holidays, or of a 32-hour, four-day week with two shifts, giving those who want it the option of working only Saturdays and Sundays in return for a full week's wage.

A politics of time which gives everyone access to a job (even part-time if they so desire) will not be the same thing as one where all that counts are the sectional interests and careers of those who have a guaranteed full-time job.[8]

A politics of liberation of time and work-sharing presupposes, at the level of each public service, sector or large company, the planning of productivity increases linked to technological development and corresponding planning of work time and staffing levels. But this planning will lead to liberation only if it is the result of continual negotiation over:

– the nature, forms and rhythm of introducing technological changes;
– the nature of jobs and the restructuring of wage and qualification scales;
– staffing levels and work time.

The conflict between different sectional interests will be overcome only by public discussion of disagreements, which can bring to light the real issues and draw out the bases for an agreement in the common interest of all the workers.

Negotiation with economic and political decision-makers will necessarily be conflictual. It will lead to freer work and a freer life only if the unions are genuinely autonomous. For business, like political administrations, will only make investments of productivity in order to lower costs (chiefly wage costs) per unit of output. But if work time is perfectly indexed to productivity and wages are kept at the same level, wage costs cannot be lowered. Economic decision-makers will thus be discouraged from investing: they will no longer have any real interest in raising productivity. If the unions wait for productivity gains in order to redistribute the profits in the form of reduced work time, there will be nothing much to redistribute.

To impose, rather than discourage, investments of productivity, reduction of work time must be taken as an independent, not a dependent, variable: it should not be the result of productivity increases, but their goal and their driving force. The unions should thus:

– impose on the economy as a whole and on each sector a plan for the reduction of work time so as to compel corresponding investments of productivity;
– participate in defining these investments;
– study the best ways of reducing capital cost per unit of output, by adopting work schedules which can make the best use of equipment (given that night work must always be prohibited). According to a non-management study in the United States,[9] the formula of a 32-hour, four-day week with two shifts (plus, if need be, Saturday-Sunday shifts paid at double time) is bound to come into general use between now and 1990 because of its advantages.

Towards a wage for life

Because of the variations in productivity growth from sector to sector, local negotiations and agreements must be co-ordinated within an overall legislative framework which can ensure the necessary adjustments and equalisations. Clearly it is unacceptable for work time to vary greatly between different sectors and different companies. Standardising work time (for example at 32 hours a week, then 28 . . .) means increasing staff levels in sectors where productivity rises slowly, lowering them where it rises rapidly. However, staff adjustments and transfers cannot be instantaneous, and variations in employment levels and a degree of flexibility of employment remain inevitable. To prevent this being synonymous with unemployment, some Swedish economists, following Gösta Rehn, advocate a definition of work time not by the month or even the year, but by five- or 10-year periods or by a whole lifetime, allowing everyone to work a little, a lot or not at all, at periods of their own choice, while still keeping their income.[10]

In effect, this system guarantees a wage for life in return for a minimum number of hours' work (which can be periodically revised) which everyone must provide during their active lifetime. Those who want a higher income can obviously work more than this minimum: all they have to do is give up some of the days, weeks or months of non-work to which a period of work entitles them.

In a refinement of this system proposed by Gunnar Adler Karlsson, everyone could choose between different life-styles matching different income levels and work intensities, with a permanent right to move from one to another – the wage for life corresponding to the performance of a minimum amount of work (currently about 20,000 hours in a lifetime) for a decent, but frugal, way of life.

In this way, necessary flexibility in work availability will be achieved without forced unemployment, by incentives to work more or less at particular times, while no voluntary interruption of activity, however long, would entail loss of wages. Comparable to a 'time-bank' system – lending time, saving time – this formula really represents the generalised application of sectoral agreements like the following:

– the agreement reached by New York dockers (in October 1976) guaranteeing no redundancies and a minimum wage of around £7,500 per annum, even if work time has been greatly reduced during the year;
– the draft collective agreement of American steelworkers which provides for 'employment for life', with a minimum lifelong wage corresponding to a 30-hour week, even if, for conjunctural or structural reasons, actual work time is less than this.

Obviously, the effectiveness of such sectoral agreements is very limited, since they only allow for work-sharing among existing full-time employees in particular sectors and do nothing to prevent subcontracting, using the army of temporary, unprotected workers. The wage-for-life system, on the contrary, redistributes all socially necessary work and all consumable production among the entire potentially active population, without restrictions.

Self-management of time

Unless we move into a war economy or new forms of institutionalised waste, the technological evolution now underway will inevitably bring a rapid drop in the duration of waged work. Provided it is shared out equally, waged work (that is, predetermined or heteronomous work) may cease to be a central occupation by the end of the century. We therefore urgently need to prepare ourselves to be active and self-employed in tasks which will be defined not by the boss, the state, the Führer or the electronic brain, but by ourselves. We have to re-learn how to devote ourselves to what we do, not because we are paid for it, but for the pleasure of creating, giving, learning, establishing with others non-market, non-hierarchic, practical and affective relationships.

For 200 years our societies have been dominated by the productivist ethic which has sanctified work as mortification and sacrifice, as a renunciation of life and pleasure, of the freedom to be oneself. It will certainly not be an easy matter to destroy it and replace it with an ethic which privileges the values of voluntary co-operation, self-determination, creativity and the quality of our relations with each other and with nature.

We should bear in mind that a lot of the men and women today who want to work, but not for 39 hours a week all year round for the rest of their lives, are quite simply opting for a lifestyle which is likely to be dominant in 10 years time. Should the union movement reject or condemn them in the name of an obsolete religion of work, it will only be harming itself. For most of the supporters of shorter working hours will never accept the glorification of waged work, will never be persuaded that work is the most important thing in life. By excluding them from the field of union action, such action will become less effective: part-time workers will be left without protection, at the employers' mercy. That is why American unions, having long ignored them, are finally coming round to accepting 'part-timers' as fully fledged union members, whose interests and rights must be defended in the common interest.

European unions' reservations, indeed hostility, towards part-timers rest on the following fear: wage demands (especially the demand for fewer hours without loss of earnings) risk being undermined by people who show they can live without a full-time wage. Employers could use them as an argument for refusing to pay a full wage for reduced work time.

More research would be needed to find out whether there are any grounds for this anxiety, and whether (as suggested in the appendix below) it could be overcome by altering union strategy. What is certain is that an 'à la carte' system of timetables and working hours does not necessarily mean playing the bosses' game. It can offer greater scope for union action – the self-management of time, in workshops, offices and departments.

In this context, the system introduced by the Beck department stores in Munich provides an interesting example. At the beginning of every month, each employee is allowed to choose his/her timetable and working hours. The only restriction on free choice is that the sum of preferences expressed must be compatible with 'departmental needs'. Quite unlike flexi-time at the employers' discretion, this formula can lead to:

– general meetings at shop and departmental level where workers themselves arbitrate between different individual preferences;
– permanent discussion of 'departmental needs', that is, of work organisation and job distribution and how these can develop in the interests of one and all;
– collective examination of the nature and effects of technological changes before they are introduced.

Finally, this self-management of time can bring the plans and ideas of the self-management movement back down to earth, to daily practice where their extension can be a spur to action, merging immediate individual interests and collective interest; a social project and a desire to live and work differently.

Appendix on part-timers

There is a very widespread desire for part-time work. According to a national survey of women by the French Ministry of Labour, 60 per cent of the six million adult women who did not have *waged* work would like a part-time job. Nearly half (47 per cent) of *all* women (employed or not) said they would prefer part-time work, as 'the only way of balancing career and family life'.

Taking this study as his starting-point, Guy Aznar (in *Part-time for All*) examines various living patterns evaluated as part of a survey he carried out for the French Government Planning Committee. He emphasises that the situation where the man works full time and the woman part time is very far from being the most popular pattern among those questioned. On the contrary, the most attractive situation is the household where both the man and the woman work part time and share domestic responsibilities. And the 'ideal' is 'man and woman both working part-time and having another *shared* activity in their free time'.

A recent survey by the Centre des Jeunes Dirigeants [Institute of Young Managers] of about 1,000 young people between 18 and 25 has just confirmed Aznar's claim: only 28.7 per cent would want 'their partner to work full time' as against 34 per cent who would rather s/he works part time. This is reaffirmed by those in professional training and, surprisingly, by 28 per cent of women. Moreover, 95 per cent of the sample judged the freedom to organise their own work time 'very important' (54 per cent) or 'important' (41 per cent).[11]

But at present this strong demand for reduced working hours, which would enable available work to be shared out among a much greater number of workers, remains almost entirely unsatisfied. Out of 1.3 million part-time jobs surveyed by the INSEE [the French National Institute for Statistics and Economic Surveys] fewer than 300,000 were permanent posts, however unskilled. Over three-quarters of the total were, in fact, those of cleaners, chars and home-helps or of casual or seasonal workers.

Only the public sector could rapidly open up more opportunities for part-time work and give the lie to the claim that such work must be menial, basically unskilled and incompatible with a professional career. There are, after all, plenty of advocates and arguments for the opposite view. Are not part-time teachers or doctors more useful to each of their pupils and patients than those who never stop working? Having the time to read, to think, to spread their interests, don't they work better by working less? In the United States and Northern Europe, the answer is obvious: in professions which demand personal investment and multiple skills, part-timers are highly appreciated.

Trade union objections, however, concern two other aspects of part-time work. It is claimed:

1. That part-timers would put up with more arduous and mindless work than full-timers. Thus they undermine the struggle for workers' control and re-skilling, for the reappropriation of work by the workers themselves.
2. That by accepting a wage cut in return for a cut in hours, part-timers undermine the struggle for shorter hours without loss of pay.

Put forward by the majority of trade unionists in almost every industrialised country, these objections are the subject of widespread, bitter debate. Their relevance is challenged by the following arguments:

– the very fact that they are paid less and need more (free) time means that part-timers have a considerable stake in the rise of hourly rates which automatically result from a *general* and *compensated* reduction of work time. Part-timers will thus be active participants in union struggles, as long as the unions themselves have not marginalised and rejected them.
– as regards the quality of work, this has been deteriorating for the last 35 years. Currently over 80 per cent of jobs fall into the unskilled category, with no room for creativity, initiative or personal investment. To believe that workers will make such debilitating work creative simply because they are compelled to do it full time is to live in a dream world. For it is precisely full-time work which stops them from ever experiencing their own potential creativity and autonomy. The liberation of time, by giving employees the chance to have a life of their own, also makes them more critical of the nature and content of their work.

By refusing to organise or give a voice to those who want more time for themselves right now, unions are only cutting themselves off from part of their own base, and strengthening the employers' power at their own expense.

Notes

Twenty-five theses towards understanding the crisis and finding a Left solution

I. What's gone forever

1. I have borrowed this term Alvin Toffler, *The Third Wave* (London, Pan Books, 1981).

2. East Germany is more industrially developed than Czechoslovakia but has not undergone a bourgeois revolution nor (apart from the years 1919–32) known parliamentary democracy.

3. Three of Rudolf Bahro's books are currently available in English: *The Alternative in Eastern Europe* (London and New York, New Left Books, 1981); *Socialism and Survival* (London, Heretic Books, 1982); *From Red to Green* (London and New York, Verso, 1984).

4. In Lenin's time, the Soviet Union was already set on borrowing the technologies of American capitalism; in the Kruschev period, on 'catching up and overtaking the United States' in per capita production and consumption.

5. It is because of these policies that hunger has been eliminated in Kerala (one of the poorest Indian states) and in Sri Lanka, where the per capita GNP is one of the lowest in the world, while it persists or even worsens in industrialising countries that are 10 times richer (according to our methods of accounting), such as Mexico or Brazil.

6. On this subject, see the work of Alvin Toffler, *op. cit.*, and Supplementary Text I, which is on his work.

II. Understanding the crisis

1. There is a clear and concise account of the trend leading up to the crisis in Manuel Castells, *Economic Crisis and American Society* (Oxford, Blackwells, 1980).

2. For more details, see the remarkably well-documented work of Denis Clerc, *Comprendre la Crise* (Paris, J.-P. Delarge, 1977,) chap. II.

3. In the *Grundrisse*, Marx uses the categories of 'fixed capital' and 'circulating capital'. In *Capital* he uses the wider concepts of 'constant capital' and 'variable capital'. The substance of his argument is the same

in both cases. Since the term 'fixed capital' is more current, I have used it here in conjunction with 'circulating capital'.

4. For a detailed discussion of this point see Philippe Ven Parijs, 'The Falling Rate-of-Profit Theory of Crisis: A Rational Reconstruction by Way of Obituary' in *The Review of Radical Political Economics* 12-1 (Spring 1980). See also Geoff Hodgson, 'The Theory of the Falling Rate of Profit', *New Left Review* 84, 1974.

5. See Michel Aglietta, *Theory of Capitalist Regulation: The US Experience* (London and New York, New Left Books, 1979); Manuel Castells and Denis Clerc, all *op. cit.*, and André Granou, Yves Barou and Bernard Billaudot in *Croissance et Crise* (Paris, Maspero, 1979), which traces the social, economic and international determinants of the present crisis.

6. See A. Granou, Y. Barou and B. Billaudot, *op. cit.*

7. These are the two aspects of what Jacques Attali calls 'production of organisation' which includes 'production of demand'. See *Les Trois Mondes* (Paris, Fayard, 1981).

8. These figures are given for West Germany by Willy Brandt in 'Mehr Beschäftigung durch weniger Arbeit', *Die Zeit*, 28, 9 July 1982.

9. See Egon Matzner, *Der Wohlfahrtsstaat von morgen* (Vienna, Österreichischer Bundesverlag, 1982), pp. 68–70.

10. Ronald Reagan's abandonment (in the summer of 1982) of his election pledge to cut welfare benefits and taxes is significant in this context.

11. According to an OECD study, the rise in *relative costs* only 'accounts for a fifth of the increase in health costs', *OECD Observer*, May 1978.

12. In *L'Ordre Cannibale* (Paris, Grasset, 1979) and *Les Trois Mondes, op. cit.*

13. *L'Ordre Cannibale, op. cit.*, pp. 200–201.

14. On medical ideology, see 'Health and Society' in A. Gorz, *Ecology as Politics* (London, Pluto Press, 1983).

15. Bruno Jobert, *Le Social en Plan* (Paris, Editions Ouvrières, 1982), p. 245.

16. Jacques Attali, *Les Trois Mondes, op. cit.*, p. 263.

17. On the theory of needs, see A. Gorz, *Strategy for Labour* (Boston, 1967) Chap. III. On the theory of poverty, see 'Ecology and Freedom' in A. Gorz, *Ecology as Politics, op. cit.*

18. *Grundrisse* (Harmondsworth, Penguin, 1973), p. 92.

19. In *Les Trois Mondes* and *L'Ordre Cannibale, op. cit.*

20. *Les Trois Mondes, op. cit.*, pp.226 and 263.

21. I have called *sphere of heteronomy* the sum of social activities which, because the producers and ultimate consumers involved remain separated by a great number of non-transparent mediations, cannot be self-determined or self-managed by those who perform them. These heteronomous activities should be taken as necessities deriving from – and

providing the material base for – the sum of activities open to self-management. Cf. A. Gorz, 'Towards a Dual Society' in *Farewell to the Working Class* (London, Pluto Press, 1982, and, Boston, South End Press, 1982).

22. In 'Can Sweden Be Shrunk?', *Development Dialogue*, 1979/2 (Dag Hammarskjöld Foundation, Uppsala), Nordal Akerman provides a closely argued model which integrates the social property of large companies with producer co-operatives and municipal administrations, each borough being responsible for covering its own basic needs – if necessary, in federation with a rural borough.

23. On the subject of the hyper-competitiveness of small workshops using new technology, supported by local co-operative services, see the excellent study by Charles F. Sabel, *Work and Politics: Division of Labour in Industry* (Cambridge University Press, 1982), p. 220 *et seq.*

24. *op. cit.*

25. Bruno Jobert, *op. cit.*, p. 251.

26. In *La Nouvelle Economie Française* (Paris, Flammarion, 1978) and *Les Trois Mondes, op. cit.*, pp. 283–9.

27. I think I was the first to point out this development in an article written in 1973, 'Socialism or Ecofascism' reprinted in *Ecology as Politics, op. cit.*

28. In *Theory of Capitalist Regulation: The US Experience, op. cit.*

29. In *Les Trois Mondes, op. cit.* pp. 117–21 and 283–97.

30. In *The Third Wave, op. cit.*

31. See on this subject Gérard Metayer, *Futurs en Tique* (Paris, Editions Ouvrières, 1982). The author shows, particularly in the last chapter, how the current telecommunications/computer system in France rules out any possibility for self-management and local democracy.

32. Cf. Jacques Attali, *L'Ordre Cannibale, op. cit.*, p. 289: 'Commodities like any others, people are exchanged and consumed by commodities, and thus are reproduced as commodities instead of as a labour force in struggle.'

33. Jacques Attali, *Les Trois Mondes, op. cit.*, pp. 296–7

III. Automation and the death of capital

1. For some examples see 'Towards a Policy of Time' in A. Gorz, *Farewell to the Working Class, op. cit.*, p. 134 *et seq.*

2. F. Vester, *Ballungsgebiete in der Krise* (Stuttgart, Deutsche Verlagsanstalt, 1976). Quoted by Ignacy Sachs in 'Quelle Crise?', *Clés*, 6 (Hachette, 1980).

3. Marx demonstrated this in the *Grundrisse* in the following way: 'If *necessary labour* had already been reduced to 1/1,000, then the total surplus value would be = 999/1,000. Now if the productive force increased a thousandfold, then *necessary labour* would decline to

1/1,000,000 of a working day and the total surplus value would amount to 999,999/1,000,000 of a working day . . . it would thus have grown by 999/1,000,000 . . . i.e. the thousandfold increase in productive force would have increased the total surplus by not even 1/1,000.' *Grundrisse*, *op. cit.*, p. 338.

4. From *The German Ideology* onwards, Marx defines communism as 'the abolition of labour and of all domination by the abolition of classes themselves', insisting that is by the *abolition* and not merely the redistribution of labour that communism is distinct from all previous revolutions.

5. *Grundrisse*, *op. cit.*, p. 709. Italicised in the original. (The Penguin translation gives the following version: 'the labour of the individual in its direct presence [is] posited as suspended individual, i.e. as social, labour.' Gorz is quoting the French translation. The original German reads: '. . . so ist andrerseits die Arbeit des Einzelnen in ihrem unmittelbaren Dasein gesetzt als aufgehoben einzelne, d. h. als gesellschaftliche Arbeit.')

6. The poverty of marxist theory has sunk to a level where, in France as in Germany, its representatives confuse socially determined, abstract labour with capitalist organisation of labour and see the abolition of skills as merely a perverse effect of the latter. This leads them to view as a rejection of marxism reflections in *Farewell to the Working Class* on the inevitable heteronomy of abstract labour.

7. The two passages from Marx to which I am referring deserve to be quoted at length: 'Indifference towards any specific kind of labour presupposes a very developed totality of real kinds of labour, of which no single one is any longer predominant . . . Indifference towards specific labours corresponds to a form of society in which individuals can with ease transfer from one labour to another, and where the specific kind is a matter of chance for them, hence of indifference. Not only the category, labour, but labour in reality has here become the means of creating wealth in general, and has ceased to be organically linked with particular individuals in any specific form. Such a state of affairs is at its most developed in the most modern form of existence of bourgeois society – in the United States. Here, then, for the first time, the point of departure of modern economics, namely the abstraction of the category "labour", "labour as such", labour pure and simple, becomes true in practice.' *Grundrisse*, *op. cit.*, pp. 104–5.

Further on, Marx notes that, 'with the suspension of the *immediate* character of living labour, as merely *individual* . . . [and] the positing of the activity of individuals as immediately general or *social* activity, the objective moments of production are stripped of this form of alienation; they are thereby posited as property, as the organic social body within which the individuals reproduce themselves as individuals, but as social individuals.' The possibility of the individual identifying with an immediately social 'general activity' whose content s/he cannot determine, is the foundation of socialist morality – which proposes loss of singularity and the merging of individual existence with social being as the highest goals and supreme virtues. This represents the greatest illusion of Marx and of marxists, and is the root of all forms of totalitarian collectivism. Cf. *Farewell to the Working Class*, 'Towards a Dual Society' and, in this volume, 'Individual, society, state'. See also the very fine essay by Ferruccio Andolfi, 'L'Utopia del Lavoro come Bisogno Vitale', in *Problemi del Socialismo*, 23, Milan, Jan–April 1982.

8. *Centre d'Etudes de l'Emploi*, Information bulletin 56, June 1982.

9. In the Netherlands, for example, unemployed youth who had never worked and who were receiving very little benefit were forbidden to do unpaid odd jobs helping the elderly: it was feared they might be taking away paid work from the employed.

10. *Insofar as* it identifies with the elite of permanent, protected workers and by so doing rejects work-sharing, flexibilisation and worker self-management of work schedules, and the re-centring of life around self-determined, non-waged activities, trade unionism is becoming a conservative force or even, in some circumstances, a reactionary one. This trend will continue unless trade unions succeed in organising, or at least supporting, the struggle of 'disaffected non-workers' (to whom I gave the name *'non-class of non-workers'* in *Farewell to the Working Class*). This would require unions to be present not only at the points of production but to give as much importance to getting people organised where they *live* as where they *work*.

11. Especially in the United States, Britain and West Germany, there have always been right-wing, or even extreme right-wing, trade unions, usually descendants of the old trade-guilds. In Latin countries, the existence of these reactionary, corporatist tendencies has been concealed by the hegemony of anarchist and marxist ideologies.

12. This dualistic model, already set out in the Nora-Minc report on *L'informatisation de la Société*, was developed in a paper by C. Soffaes and J. Amado, *Vers une Socio-Economie Duale?* (La Documentation Française, 1980). The model outlined by Alain Minc in *L'Après-Crise a Commencé* (Paris, Gallimard, 1982) follows this conception, envisaging different sectors and different lifestyles, but implictly excludes the possibility of belonging to two sectors simultaneously. Moreover, these sectors, in Minc's version, are dominated by market relations and capitalist logic.

13. Guy Aznar, *Tous à Mi-Temps* (Paris, Editions du Seuil, 1981). Aznar uses the term 'spatial' for a dualistic division in which the population is segregated into one sector *or* the other, and the term 'temporal' for one in which everyone divides their time between the two sectors.

14. See thesis 11 above.

15. *Les Trois Mondes*, *op. cit.*, p. 291.

16. Jacques Attali, *L'Ordre Cannibale*, *op. cit.*, pp.251–3.

17. *op. cit.*, pp. 256–7.

18. A plausible description of computerized society can be found in John Brunner's novel, *Shockwave Rider*, (London, Futura, 1977).

19. Cf. thesis 13 above.

20. Jacques Attali evokes this process without drawing the political conclusions when he talks of 'new specialists who are planning new methods of business management and programming the new networks of demand production. These new specialists in social organisation plan and produce everything from television programmes to parks to the software of autosurveillance. They are members of the new ruling class and have control over a significant proportion of created value [?]. They can already be found within the state machinery and the big multinationals. These technicians, who mould and manipulate demand production, are partially replacing the existing dominant strata in industrial society.' *La Nouvelle Economie Française* (Paris, Flammarion, 1978), p. 151.

21. 'For there to be technocracy,' writes Touraine, 'a system of means must become its own end, which implies that it is given a function of domination, manipulation, and repression . . . The ruling class is the identification of science and technology production with an apparatus monopolising a certain type of information. Class domination consists in running a collectivity in such a way as to strengthen the apparatus of control.' Alain Touraine, 'Crise ou Mutation?' in *Au-delà de la Crise* (Paris, Editions du Seuil, 1976).

IV. A way out of capitalism

1. Founded by Major C.H. Douglas, the Social Credit Movement still has followers among the liberal technocracy in Britain, Canada and New Zealand. See Keith Roberts, *Automation, Unemployment and the Distribution of Income* (European Centre for Work and Society, Maastricht, 1982).

2. See OECD, *Negative Income Tax* (Paris, 1974).

3. A reduction of work time by an average of about 2 per cent per year would lead to about 900 working hours per year by the end of the century.

4. Work time could be reduced to 20,000 hours a year right away if, as a hypothesis, the citizens of the 1980s were able to opt for the consumption levels of the 1960s.

The current work time of the waged, active population (allowing for leave and holidays, partial or full unemployment, retraining, etc.) is about 40,000 hours per lifetime for an average *disposable* income of around £1,000 per household per month in 1980.

5. The adjustment of output to needs will thus not be achieved by 'market forces': effective needs, like production levels, must be determined through research and planning. Of necessity, market logic will disappear along with that of the law of value.

6. According to Marx, this principle characterises *communist* society which is both the completion and the supersession of *socialist* society.

7. The term 'social wage' was invented by the far Left in Italy at the end of the 1960s. The British Social Credit Movement of the 1920s used 'social dividend' to indicate that each citizen was a co-owner of the entire productive apparatus. The term 'social income' was coined at the beginning of the 1930s by Jacques Duboin, whose movement for a distributive economy offers the most developed social and institutional model for superseding market relations. Duboin's published texts can still be obtained from *La Grande Relève*, 88 boulevard Carnot, 78110 Le Vésinet, France.

8. See especially G. Rehn, 'For Greater Flexibility of Working Life' in *OECD Observer*, 62, Feb. 1973, and *Towards a Society of Free Choice* (Swedish Institute for Social Research, 1978).

9. Gunnar Adler-Karlsson, 'The Unimportance of Full Employment', English résumé in *IFDA Dossier 2*, Nov. 1978, Foundation internationale pour une autre développement, Nyon (Suisse), of *Tankar om den fulla sysselsättningen*, Stockholm, 1977.

10. I am paraphrasing the *Grundrisse*, p.704.

11. See 'Towards a Policy of Time' in *Farewell to the Working Class*, *op. cit.*

12. See in this context a very interesting book from a business economist: J.-L. Michau, *L'Horaire Modulaire* (Paris, Masson/ Institut de l'entreprise, 1981).

13. On this subject see the powerful account by Charly Boyadjian in Adret, *Travailler Deux Heures par Jour* (Paris, Editions du Seuil, 1977) and *La Nuit des Machines*. The author, a worker in a large shoemaking factory, tells how the introduction of a 32-hour week led the workers to refuse to accept what they had previously tolerated when working a 48-hour week, and helped them rediscover the importance of comradeship, love and militancy, while reducing their concern for consumption and standard of living.

14. I have already emphasised this point in *Farewell to the Working Class*. The disciples of the religion of work generally did not notice this, being too busy defending their (unattainable, regressive) desire to make waged work the permanent centre of everyone's life.

15. This was admirably demonstrated by the Ricardian socialist Thomas Hodgskin in *Labour Defended Against the Claims of Capital* (London, 1825), which Marx quotes in the *Grundrisse*, p. 709: ' "As soon as the

division of labour is developed, almost every piece of work done by a single individual is a part of a whole, *having no value or utility of itself. There is nothing on which the labourer can seize: this is my produce, this I will keep to myself.*" ' It should be emphasised that *alienation*, in Marx, as in Sartre, defines the becoming-other *for myself* of *my* activity when its process and its result are themselves the *materials* of others' labour (which is always the case, to some extent): I can no longer recognise myself as the author of my deeds. The reference to alienation in no way implies a reference to the individual as s/he would have existed *before* all alienation. This *before* is absolutely inconceivable. As I have shown at length elsewhere (in *Fondements pour une Morale* and in *The Traitor* (London, John Calder, 1960), childhood is an original condition of alienation. The different forms of alienation can be limited and superseded but never removed.

16. Marx distinguished the 'accidental' or 'natural' division of tasks where an individual is restricted to this or that job without any choice, from the 'voluntary division' through 'voluntary co-operation'. See *The German Ideology* (London, Lawrence and Wishart, 1964).

17. Cf. *Farewell to the Working Class*, 'The Post-Industrial Revolution'.

18. Cf. *Farewell to the Working Class*, 'Towards a Dual Society'.

19. I have developed these remarks on the oppressive nature of tightly integrated communities and on the emancipatory, enriching potential of external, heteronomous work, in *Farewell to the Working Class*, 'The Sphere of Necessity: The State'.

20. On job-sharing in highly qualified professions, see the examples in *Farewell to the Working Class*, 'Towards a Policy of Time', p. 141 *et seq.*

21. *Farewell to the Working Class*, 'Towards a Dual Society'.

22. For more details, see 'Socialism or Ecofascism' in *Ecology as Politics, op. cit.*, and 'Utopia for a Possible Dual Society' in *Farewell to the Working Class*.

23. *Grundrisse, op. cit.*, p. 706 *et seq.* (Marx, however, does not give the full title of the pamphlet, nor do the bibliographies of the German, French or English editions. *Tr.*)

24. *The Source and Remedy of the National Difficulties Deduced from Principles of Political Economy in a Letter to Lord John Russell* (London, Rodwell and Martin, 1821).

25. Cf. 'Utopia for a Possible Dual Society' in *Farewell to the Working Class.*

26. See Charles Sabel, *Work and Politics: Division of Labour in Industry, op. cit.*

27. Cf. the remarks on the internalisation of social costs in thesis 10, I above.

28. In *Can Sweden be Shrunk?*, *op. cit.*

29. See Edgar Morin, *La Vie de la Vie* (Paris, Editions du Seuil, 1980), p. 325.

Supplementary Texts

I. 'The Third Wave' according to Alvin Toffler
1. *The Third Wave*, *op. cit.*
2. On this whole question, see the remarkable work of Ingmar Gransted, a former industrial executive turned academic, *L'Impasse Industrielle* (Paris, Editions du Seuil, 1980).
3. On this subject, see the classic study by David Riesman and Nathan Glazer, *The Lonely Crowd* (New York, 1951).
4. The possible transition to a society based on voluntary co-operation to deal with, in the case of Sweden, in the remarkable study by Nordal Akerman, *Can Sweden be Shrunk?*, *op. cit.*

II. Their famine, our food
1. The documentation in this article is largely drawn from the remarkable range of material gathered by Frères des Hommes and Terre des Hommes. Further information can be obtained from Frères des Hommes, 20, rue du Refuge, 78 Versailles, France.
2. In particular, see Claude Aubert, *Une Autre Assiette: Conseils pratiques pour une alimentation saine, simple, savoureuse et économique* (Editions Debard, 17, rue du Vieux-Colombier, Paris 6, France), and Frances Moore Lappé, *Sans Viande et Sans Regret* (Edition de l'Etincelle, Montreal, Quebec).
3. See Bernard Lambert, *Les Paysans dans la Lutte des Classes* (Paris, Editions du Seuil).
4. See Stella and Joël de Rosnay, *La Malbouffe* (Paris, Edition Olivier Orban).
5. On the advantages of stock-rearing on temporary pasture, see the scientifically sophisticated report of a Breton stock-breeder, André Pochon, 'Trèfle Blanc' (Institut technique de l' élevage bovin, 149, rue de Bercy, 75595 Paris, France).
6. See note 1.

III. Automation and the politics of time
1. See Mike Cooley, 'Les Microprocesseurs ou les Hommes?' in *Actes du Colloque International Informatique et Société*, Vol. II, pp. 245–62 (La Documentation Française, 1980) and 'The Taylorisation of Intellectual Work' in *Science, Technology and the Labour Process* (London, CSE Books, 1981).

2. See on this subject the remarkable thesis of Guy Caire, 'Automation: technologie, travail, relations sociales' in Adefi, *Les Mutations Technologiques*, pp. 165–94 (Economica, 1981).

3. Sir Adrian Cadbury, one of the most 'progressive' industrialists in Europe, predicted that most people will want their work to fit into their lives and not the other way round and that the efficiency of their work will depend on how much they are allowed to be involved in it, on how much influence they can have over their company's decisions and aims. The company would have to be relatively small for this to be possible. (The *Guardian*, 9.12.81.)

4. Interview with Michel Rolant in *Le Nouvel Observateur*, 21 May 1979. Until 1981 Michel Rolant was deputy head of CFDT, where he was responsible for economic issues.

5. This is the idea of a 'third sector' put forward by Jacques Delors. See, in particular, 'Echanges et Projets' in *La Démocratie à la Portée de la Main* (1977).

6. Numerous examples of autoproduction can be found in Guy Aznar, *Tous à Mi-Temps*, *op. cit.*

7. In *Can Sweden be Shrunk?*, *op. cit.*

8. The journal *Futuribles*, October 1981, gives three models of a politics of time. The same national output can be achieved by 98 per cent of permanent employees working 31 hours a week, or at the other extreme, by 50 per cent of temporary employees working a maximum of a six months a year, 14 per cent of part-time employees and 30 per cent of full-time employees working 40 hours a week.

9. Delphi poll organised by the University of Michigan and the Society of Manufacturing Engineers, 1978. Cited in Joël Le Quément, *Les Robots, Enjeux Economiques et Sociaux* (La Documentation Française, 1981).

10. See Guy Aznar, *op. cit.*

11. See the March 1982 edition of *Dirigeant*, journal of the Centre des Jeunes Dirigeants (CJD), 19, avenue George-V, Paris.